BACKROADS
SOUTHERN INTERIOR
BRITISH COLUMBIA

BACK ROADS

Southern Interior British Columbia

JOAN DONALDSON-YARMEY

LONE PINE

To Tylar and Brittany

THE PUBLISHER
LONE PINE PUBLISHING

206, 10426-81 Avenue	202A, 1110 Seymour Street	16149 Redmond Way, #180
Edmonton, Alberta	Vancouver, British Columbia	Redmond, Washington
Canada T6E 1X5	Canada V6B 3N3	U.S.A. 98052

Canadian Cataloguing in Publication Data

Donaldson-Yarmey, Joan, 1949-
    Backroads of Southern Interior British Columbia

    Includes bibliographical references and index.
    ISBN 1-55105-070-6

1. Automobile travel—British Columbia—Guidebooks.
2. British Columbia—Guidebooks. I. Title.
FC3807.D66 1996   917.1104'4   C96-910337-9
F1087.D66 196

Senior Editor: Nancy Foulds
Editorial: Jennifer Keane, Volker Bodegom
Design: Bruce Timothy Keith
Maps: Volker Bodegom
Layout: Volker Bodegom, Greg Brown, Bruce Timothy Keith, Carol S. Dragich
Printing: Quebecor Jasper Printing, Edmonton, Alberta, Canada

All photos by the Author unless otherwise noted.

The Publisher gratefully acknowledges the support of Alberta Community Development, the Department of Canadian Heritage and the Canada/Alberta Agreement on Cultural Industries.

CONTENTS

ACKNOWLEDGEMENTS

In the time I spent travelling 9000 kilometres (5400 miles) through this part of British Columbia, I drove all the highways and many of the gravelled, high mountain, back country roads. All these backroads are narrow and winding and have steep climbs and sharp drop-offs. While on some of them, I wondered if I would make it back down. Although it was sometimes scary, driving those roads was truly breathtaking and exhilarating.

What really impressed me most about BC highways is that there is little or no garbage along them. It definitely makes for a more pleasant visit.

I met many wonderful people on my trip who were willing to answer my questions, give me directions, tell me about their area, and take me to out-of-the-way sites. To these people go my heartfelt thanks for helping me make this book possible.

INTRODUCTION

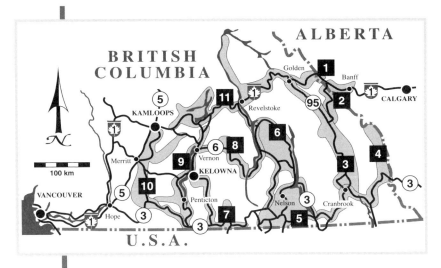

British Columbia is one of the most scenic provinces in Canada. It has mountains, canyons, lakes, rivers, forests, open ranges and arid lands. Every time you drive over a hill or around a curve you will see some new and amazing scenery until you finally run out of words to describe it. Much has been done to make it possible for residents and visitors to enjoy the province's richness and history.

The government has made sure that every road has provincial parks, rest areas, picnic sites, viewpoints and hiking trails. The people of the province have provided museums, summer and winter resorts, crafts shops, restaurants, attractions, golf courses, adventures and festivals. These features are too numerous to name all in this book, so only the most unusual or unique have been included. The rest you will have to discover yourself.

This book is for residents who want to see some of the province they haven't visited before. It is also for visitors who are here on holiday and want to see as much as possible in the time allowed. *Backroads of Southern Interior British Columbia* does not claim to tell everything there is to see and do on each road. It does, however, take you down every highway and up some high mountain, back country trails in the southern Interior, and gives you something different to see on these roads. Through it you will learn about the history, the natural and man-made attractions, and the famous, or not so famous, people of the area.

You can access southern Interior British Columbia from many different directions. You could come via Lake Louise (Chapter 1), Banff (Chapter 2) or the Crowsnest (Chapter 4), or by Kamloops (Chapter 11), or other routes that connect to the highways in the area.

The book is divided into sections that could be driven in a day. Each section is as closely connected to the next as possible to make travelling around this part of the province easy and enjoyable. Unless otherwise stated, the odometer is reset to zero at the last building as you leave each town. However, most places mentioned in this book have highway signs indicating their turn-off. For those that don't, landmarks are given to let you know when you are approaching the turn. A main map for the roads described in each chapter is provided at the beginning of the chapter to give you an idea of how your trip is laid out, and additional maps with greater detail are provided as necessary. Bring along other maps – from government, motor associations or local tourism authorities – to help with an overall view of the regions this book covers.

This part of the province is mountainous, so you will be doing a lot of driving up and down hills. Make sure that your vehicle is in good condition, especially if you are pulling a trailer. Also, because of the terrain, many hiking trails have steep sections. Be certain you are in good enough shape for the climb before starting out.

CHAPTER 1
LAKE LOUISE TO GOLDEN

Emerald Lake

CHAPTER 1
LAKE LOUISE TO GOLDEN

Many people begin their journey into British
Columbia along Highway 1 via Lake Louise,
Alberta. Sights to take in on this route include
Lake Louise itself, Lake Agnes and Moraine Lake.
Highway 1 through Yoho National Park is only
67 kilometres (42 miles) long but there is a lot
to see along it.

LAKE LOUISE

Chateau Lake Louise

The village of Lake Louise is small and scenic with the Bow River flowing through it. It has all services, including a trailer drop-off lot on Sentinel Road. You might want to leave your trailer there rather than pull it over the narrow roads to the lakes. To see all of the valley scenery, take the gondola ride up Whitehorn Mountain.

At the four-way stop in the village of Lake Louise are signs pointing west to Lake Louise itself. At kilometre 2.2 (mile 1.4) you come to the junction to Moraine Lake. The road to Lake Louise is steep and has many pot-holes. During the height of the tourist season it is bumper-to-bumper traffic. You can expect the parking lot to be crowded and you may have to walk a distance to the chateau and lake.

LAKE LOUISE

Lake Louise is 2.4 kilometres (1.5 miles) long, less than 0.5 kilometre (0.3 mile) wide and 75 metres (250 feet) deep. It is formed from the melting of the Victoria Glacier. Its outlet is a stream that flows to the Bow River.

The first non-Native to see the lake was a CPR worker named Tom Wilson. Indian guides took him to it in 1882 and he immediately named it Emerald Lake because of its colour. It was renamed Louise in 1884 to honour the fourth daughter of Queen Victoria, Princess Louise Caroline Alberta. The province of Alberta was also named after her.

Lake Louise, as well as the other glacier-fed lakes and rivers in the mountains, gets its colour from rock flour (fine particles that are brought down in the meltwaters from the glaciers and remain suspended in the lake).

The Canadian Pacific Railway (CPR) constructed a one-storey log building in 1890 and quickly followed it with a large, Tudor-style chateau. One of the wings was made of concrete; it was all that survived when the hotel burned in 1924. The 375-room Chateau Lake Louise you now see is made of brick and has been here since 1924.

A shoreline trail leads from Chateau Lake Louise to the other end of the lake. Longer hiking trails lead higher into the mountains. If you take the trail to Lake Agnes you can refresh yourself at the teahouse there before returning. Although the hiking will warm you up, bring along an extra sweater or jacket because the winds at the higher altitude can be chilly.

MORAINE LAKE

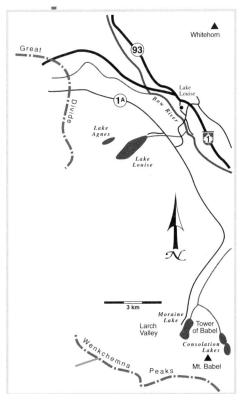

On your way back from Lake Louise, turn onto the road to Moraine Lake. Many people claim that Moraine Lake closely rivals Lake Louise for beauty but hasn't been commercialized yet.

The road is narrow and rough in places. The climb is gradual and traffic is not heavy. You drive through fir and spruce, and along the way are beautiful views of the Bow Valley. At kilometre 9 (mile 5.6) from the junction, you will see the Wenkchemna Peaks. Wenkchemna is the Stoney Indian word for 'ten,' and the lake is set in the Valley of the Ten Peaks. Between the peaks are avalanche chutes that occasionally send debris sliding to the water's edge.

Moraine Lake is the same lovely colour as Lake Louise. For a better view, climb up the Tower of Babel. Over the centuries, rock fell from the nearby Mount Babel and slowly built the hill. As it grew, the tower eventually dammed the run-off from the moun-

Trail up to the top of Tower of Babel

tains and Moraine Lake was formed. It is an easy climb to the top. Be sure to stop and read the interpretive signs.

Or if you are romantic, rent a canoe and drift over the beautiful blue-green waters.

The Moraine Lake area is a hiker's paradise, but at 1900 metres (6230 feet) above sea level, many of the trails might still have snow on them in June. One trail, to Consolation Lake, is 3.2 kilometres (2 miles) and takes about an hour. If you are lucky enough to be in the mountains in the autumn, take the 3 kilometre (1.8 mile) trail that begins behind the Moraine Lake Lodge to Larch Valley. Here you will see the colourful splendour as the larch needles change from green to gold. This species is the only conifer that sheds it needles in the fall. Larch Valley is a photographer's delight.

Moraine Lake, with the jagged peaks behind, is on the back of our $20 bills. The names of the ten peaks are Mount Fay on the left, then working your way right, Little, Bowlen, Perren, Septa, Allen, Tuzo, Deltaform (the highest), Neptuak and Wenkchemna.

YOHO NATIONAL PARK

Great Divide on Highway 1A

There are two ways to get to Yoho National Park from Lake Louise. You can take Highway 1 west of the town and stay on it as it heads into Yoho, or you can take the road back up towards Lake Louise and watch for the sign that says 'Field, 27 kilometres.' Take that road and you will be going on the old highway (1A). It is a more relaxing, scenic route although the road is narrower. In 7 kilometres (4.3 miles), you reach the Great Divide at 1625 metres (5331 feet) above sea level.

The Great Divide, or Continental Divide, is the border between British Columbia and Alberta and is marked by a huge log archway. 'British Columbia' is painted on one side and 'Alberta' on the other. There is a picnic area here with a monument near the railway tracks. Watch for tour buses stopping here to let their passengers take pictures of the arch. When you go under the arch you are entering British Columbia and Yoho National Park.

At kilometre 9.9 (mile 6.1) is the turn-off to Lake O'Hara. Lake O'Hara is a small lake surrounded by splendid castellated mountains. There are 25 lakes and 80 kilometres (50 miles) of hiking trails in the vicinity. However, access to the area is controlled to protect its extreme fragility. There is a 13 kilometre (8 mile) walk in to Lake O'Hara but many people prefer to pay a small fee and take the bus rides offered each day.

You can camp at the Parks Canada campground or stay in the luxurious, privately owned Lake O'Hara Lodge.

At kilometre 10 (mile 6.2) you reach the new highway. Turn left.

If you take Highway 1, instead of 1A, from Lake Louise you will come to the junction with Highway 93; 7 kilometres (4.3 miles) west of the junction is the entrance to Yoho. Kilometre 2.5 (mile 1.5) from that entrance is where Highway 1A joins Highway 1.

Old Bridge on Big Hill

The gradual climb to Kicking Horse Pass is beside the channels of the Bow River. As you continue along Highway 1 you pass the West Louise Lodge and Kicking Horse Service Centre and Junk Food, and reach the turn-off to Wapta Lake. Watch for Sherbrooke Creek Falls on the right at kilometre 6.5 (mile 4). The creek runs under the road and beside it on the left. One kilometre (0.6 mile) from there is the Old Bridge on Big Hill.

This stone bridge is a remnant of the first CPR route through the Kicking Horse Pass. The tracks on Big Hill had the sharpest descent in North America. They dropped 400 metres (1310 feet) in the 10 kilometres (6 miles) between the Continental Divide and the floor of the valley. After the Spiral Tunnels were constructed, this bridge and railway bed were used as part of the highway through the park. You can turn in and walk on the old bridge if you wish.

STEEP GRADE

Despite several inclines of 4.5% – which means a drop of 4.5 metres per 100 metres distance (or 4.5 feet per 100 feet) – on the B.C. side, the CPR built tracks through the Kicking Horse Pass in 1884. Big Hill became noted for having the sharpest grade in North America. It dropped 400 metres (1312 feet) from the Continental Divide. The first train to descend the grade lost control and derailed, killing three men.

There was a limit to the number of train cars that could be pulled up the slope or run down the grade. It took four engines to pull a train up the hill. To lessen the steepness, the CPR constructed the Spiral Tunnels through two mountains in 1909.

Workers cut an 887 metre (2910 foot) tunnel through Mount Ogden and a 992 metre (3255 foot) tunnel through Cathedral Mountain so that the track looped slowly downward and cut the grade to 2.2%.

Just past the bridge is the turn-off for the Lower Spiral Tunnel viewpoint. Watch to your right as you are turning in and you will see a section of track coming down the mountainside. It shows how steep the grade is even with the new tunnels. Follow the path at the far end of the parking lot onto a replica of an old wooden train trestle. There is a viewpoint at the end where you can read up on the history of the Spiral Tunnels and watch a train wind its way through Mount Ogden. Or if no train is coming, view the lovely Yoho Valley to the right.

The Yoho Valley Road, which leads to Takakkaw Falls, is paved and takes you from the broad valley of the Kicking Horse River through the narrow, steep-walled Yoho River valley before reaching the falls. The drive is 13 kilometres (8 miles) and if you are pulling a trailer, you should leave it in the drop-off area across from the Kicking Horse Overflow.

Just after you cross the Kicking Horse River you will come to a viewpoint. From it you can see the CPR's Upper Spiral Tunnels in Cathedral Mountain above you.

Within another kilometre (0.6 mile) you will come to the Meeting of the Waters viewpoint, from which you can see the raging junction of the Yoho and Kicking Horse rivers. The waters of the Yoho are milky from the meltwater of nearby glaciers, while the Kicking Horse waters are clearer because most of the silt has settled out in upstream lakes before reaching this point. To get a better picture of the joining, walk along the path from the picnic tables. The path is over tree roots and eventually you will be able to see the confluence through the trees.

Takakkaw Falls

From the meeting, the road continues through the narrow valley of the Yoho River. Watch for the two 180° switchbacks in about 2 kilometres (1.2 miles). To make the second one you will have to back up halfway through.

You will be able to see the falls on the mountain side before you reach the parking lot. While standing in the lot you can see the top half of Takakkaw Falls; to see the total height follow the asphalt path to the right. It is a short walk and you cross a bridge over the Yoho River then follow the stream made by the falls to the base.

Natural Bridge over Kicking Horse River

Takakkaw is a Cree word meaning 'it is wonderful' or 'magnificent' and the Cree were right. The falls have a total drop of 503 metres (1650 feet), making them the highest falls in North America. The waters that cascade down the rock wall emanate from the Daly Glacier and the nearby Waputik Icefield.

If you feel in the mood for a little exercise and want to see more falls, follow the 9 kilometre (5.6 mile) path from the parking area up the Yoho Valley. Depending on how far you walk, you will encounter Laughing Falls, Point Lace Falls, Angel's Staircase Falls and Twin Falls. The Twin Falls teahouse was built in 1900 by the CPR and tourists could only reach it by horseback. It still keeps its rustic atmosphere. There is no running water or power and all supplies are packed in. Light lunches and hot tea are served until 4:30 pm, and overnight accommodation is available but the rooms have three or four beds each. You will be given hot water for washing and the outdoor toilets are a walk away from the chalet.

Tenters who wish to spend the night beside a waterfall can take the three minute walk from the parking lot to the Takakkaw Falls Walk-in Campground. Because of the rugged terrain, large wooden pallets have been built for you to set your tent up on. From the campground you have a magnificent view of the falls and the sound of the water roaring over the rock is relaxing.

Back on Highway 1 you follow the channels of the Kicking Horse River to the turn-off into Field and the Park Information Centre. As you leave the highway you cross a bridge over the river and turn right.

There is a large parking lot and beside the lot is a small pond with a few tables around it and a playground. Watch for the flock of Canada geese wandering around the far end. Inside the Information Centre are displays of the Burgess Shale fossils, which have made Yoho

Inside Field Information Centre

famous. The mudslides that buried the living sea creatures 530 million years ago have preserved them in amazing detail. They were selected as a World Heritage Site in 1981.

The fossil beds were discovered in 1909 by paleontologist Charles Doolittle Walcott. You won't be able to visit the actual fossil beds on your own. They are closed to the public to protect the area, but if you wish to see them, you can sign up for a guided tour to Mount Stephen. There is also an exhibit at the base of Mount Field at the Kicking Horse Campground 5 kilometres (3 miles) south of Field.

If you are biking or backpacking and the day is cool, warm up beside the wood stove set in a small room in the Information Centre.

YOHO NATIONAL PARK

At 1313 square kilometres (507 square miles) Yoho National Park is the second smallest park in the Canadian Rockies. The Trans-Canada Highway (Highway 1) is the only road through the park, although it has numerous hiking trails.

There are 28 mountains with heights of over 3000 metres (9800 feet). The highest is Mount Goodsir, which is 3562 metres (11,686 feet) above sea level. There are two different types of mountains in the park. At the east entrance are the Eastern Main Ranges with their impressive cliffs and great heights. These mountains are made up of limestone and erosion-resistant quartzose sandstone, hence their stateliness.

Once you reach the village of Field in British Columbia, you come to the Western Main Ranges, which are made of limestone interspersed with softer rocks such as shale. Time has eroded away these jagged peaks, leaving a much softer looking mountain.

More than 600 different types of plants have been identified in the park, and animals range in size from heather voles to grizzly bears. Over 200 species of bird make their homes in the park during the year.

Emerald Lake

Watch for the turn-off to the Natural Bridge and Emerald Lake. The Natural Bridge was once a Kicking Horse River waterfall. Erosion caused by the limestone in the water plus the grinding of grit and sand cut holes in the bedrock beneath the waterfall and eventually the river started flowing under the rock instead of over it.

You can walk on a bridge over the river to a viewpoint where you can see the water rushing under the rock. You will be able to see how the Kicking Horse River is cutting down its bed and deepening the valley it has created.

WORLD HERITAGE SITE

In 1972, the United Nations Educational, Scientific and Cultural Organization (UNESCO), in an effort to preserve the world's natural and man-made heritage, formed the World Heritage Committee; Canada joined on July 26, 1976.

A World Heritage Site is a place or property that is deemed to have outstanding universal cultural or natural merit. Properties that fall under the cultural site category are monuments, groups of buildings, and sites. Natural properties are formations, habitats of threatened plants or animals, and sites of natural beauty or those that benefit science and conservation.

Yoho and Kootenay national parks in British Columbia and Banff and Jasper national parks in Alberta make up the Canadian Rocky Mountain Parks, which was placed on the list in 1983 as a Natural Site. The Burgess Shale fossil site in Yoho National Park had been accepted separately in 1981, but was added to the parks property.

Banff National Park was established in 1885 and was the forerunner of Canada's national parks system. Yoho was added in 1886, Jasper in 1907 and Kootenay in 1920. Together, these parks make up one of the world's largest protected natural areas. They have as many as 60 different species of mammal, one of the world's important fossil sites (Burgess Shale), steep valleys carved by glaciers, tall mountain peaks, deep blue lakes, hot springs and magnificent scenery.

The parks offer Canada and the world outstanding natural heritage to be preserved and enjoyed for many years to come.

Emerald Lake is a beautiful emerald green. You can eat your lunch at the picnic area or take the short 0.7 kilometre (0.4 mile) hike from the parking lot to Hamilton Falls. A longer hike is the easy 5.2 kilometre (3.2 mile) self-guided trail around the lake. If it is early in the morning or just growing dark, watch for moose feeding as you walk.

Botanists might want to take the Emerald Basin trail and see the western hemlock, the most common tree on the Alaskan and northern B.C. coasts, and western redcedar, which generally likes lower elevations and moist soils. If you want to look for more exotic trees, watch for the western white pine, a tree that lives from moist valleys to dry slopes and sometimes up to the subalpine, and the western yew, which is usually found in coastal areas.

If you want to let someone else do the walking, book a horseback ride at the stables just before the parking lot. You can take an hour or an all-day ride. Or rent a canoe for a nice paddle around the lake.

Emerald Lake was the setting used on the backs of Canadian 10 dollar bills between 1954 and 1971.

Wildhorse River

As you drive along Highway 1 watch for the river valley on your right. At kilometre 9 (mile 5.6) from the Emerald Lake turn-off you come to Ottertail Viewpoint, where you can see the Kicking Horse River valley below. The river is more green than blue, a kind of green-turquoise.

If you decide to stay the night in the park, try the Hoodoos Creek Campground. While there, take the short but steep 3.2 kilometre (2 mile) walk to the Leanchoil Hoodoos. These hoodoos were formed when the softer layers of the piles of glacial debris were cut down by erosion. The tops, made up of harder rock, became caps which then protected the softer materials directly beneath them, leaving the columns standing alone.

The beginning of the trail is level, but after crossing the footbridge over the Hoodoos Creek, you begin a steep climb. There are some switchbacks and great views of the river below and the mountains across the valley. At the river crossing is a sign explaining the formation of the hoodoos.

One kilometre (0.6 mile) from the campground is the road to Wapta Falls. You will not see a highway sign from this way because the turn-off from the highway is too dangerous from this direction. You will have to drive to the exit of the park, turn around, and come back. The trailhead is 1.6 kilometres (1 mile) from the turn-off going south on the access road. The hiking trail is 2.3 kilometres (1.4 miles) long. Wapta Falls is as wide as the river and 30 metres (98 feet) high. It is situated on a bend in the Kicking Horse River.

For canoeists and kayakers, the Kicking Horse River is a Grade II water between the joining with the Amiskwi River and the Trans-Canada Highway bridge near Chancellor Peak Campground at the south end of the park. (See p. 51 for river grades.)

If you like winter camping, you will need a free permit. A small booklet, also free, provides a map of the designated cross-country ski trails of the park. Check the current snow and avalanche conditions at the Information Centre before starting out.

After leaving the park you go through a series of curves, which can be slippery if wet or frosty. You cross the Kicking Horse River twice and drive beside its narrow, steep canyon. Twenty-four kilometres (15 miles) from the park you look down on Golden.

CHAPTER 2
BANFF TO RADIUM HOT SPRINGS

Path to Radium Hot Springs

BANFF TO RADIUM HOT SPRINGS

Although Banff is not a part of British Columbia,
most people who enter the province from the east,
or leave in that direction, stop at Banff. The town
is the biggest attraction in the Canadian Rockies.
Hikers will like Kootenay National Park for its
many trails into lakes, mountains and glaciers.
The highway follows the Vermilion River and then
the Kootenay River through the park.

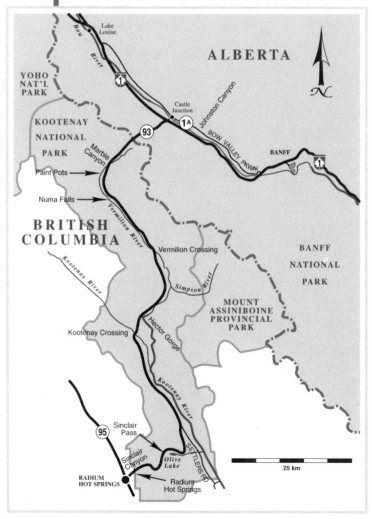

BANFF TO KOOTENAY NATIONAL PARK

Cave and Basin

Banff could be called the most visited town in Canada. During the summer, millions of people stroll its streets looking for the right souvenir or just taking in the sights. If you visit during those months, expect wall-to-wall people. If you wish to have more space and less hassle, make your trip during June or September.

Banff began as Siding 29 along the Canadian Pacific Railway (CPR) tracks in 1883. When Banff National Park was formed, Siding 29 moved about 3 kilometres (1.9 miles) west to its present site and was named after Banffshire in Scotland, the birthplace of CPR president George Stephen. Banff is the oldest and largest town in the mountain parks.

Banff Avenue runs the length of the town; every attraction can be reached from Banff Avenue. The first attraction to visit is the Cave and Basin Hot Springs. This hot springs was the reason that Banff National Park was formed, thus beginning Canada's national parks system. Go south on Banff Avenue, cross the bridge over the Bow River and turn right at the set of lights. You will be on Cave Avenue. Follow it past the residential area to the parking lot at the springs.

Enter the Cave and Basin Centennial Centre and for a small fee you will be able to walk through the lighted tunnel built in the rock to the Cave. At the Cave, natural light streams in from the hole in the ceiling through which the discoverers of the springs entered. In the early days, bathers would climb down into the Cave by means of a ladder from that hole. There is a bench for you to sit on and enjoy the calming effect of the water gurgling out of the wall into the small pool.

Also inside the centre are exhibits, a mural depicting the men lowering themselves on a rope into the cave, and a slide show about the discovery of the Cave and Basin and formation of the national park.

Outside are a number of hiking trails. The Discovery Boardwalk Trail takes you above the Cave and Basin to see the early entrance into the Cave pool – a hole in the ground. The Marsh Boardwalk Trail leads you through the wetlands below the Cave and Basin.

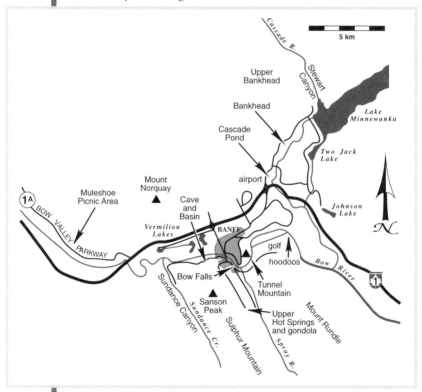

Upper Hot Springs in Banff

Signs along it explain how warm run-off from the Sulphur Mountain hot springs keep the plants growing all year.

The longest of these trails is to Sundance Canyon. You walk 4.8 kilometres (3 miles) to the picnic area. From there the trail itself is a 2.4 kilometre (1.5 mile) loop and begins at the end of the road. It passes under an overhanging cliff, rises beside the creek's cascades, and crosses from side to side on wooden bridges. Stone steps guide you upwards and when you cross the creek for the last time and reach the fork, take the path to the right. The path climbs gradually away from the canyon and takes you through tall stands of trees to a lookout over the Bow Valley. From here you descend back to the road and the return walk to your vehicle.

The Luxton Museum is on your left as you return to the lights on Banff Avenue. It has one of Alberta's finest collections of Plains Indian artifacts. You can see their daily life depicted and can buy some Native crafts and jewellery from the gift shop. The stone building on the right is the Park Administration headquarters. The beautiful Cascade Gardens, established during the Depression, are behind the building.

To reach the Upper Hot Springs or the top of Sulphur Mountain, go through the set of lights. Get into the right lane and turn onto Mountain Avenue uphill past the Park Administration building. If you want to see the Cascade Gardens, watch for the parking area to the right as you turn onto Mountain Avenue. At the end of the avenue is a fork in the road. To the right

Gondola, Banff

is the Upper Hot Springs. To the left is the Sulphur Mountain Gondola Lift.

There are eight different springs on the face of Sulphur Mountain. With a maximum temperature of 47°C (117°F) the Upper Hot Springs is the warmest. Don't try swimming in it – just lay back and enjoy.

The gondola will take you to the summit ridge, which is 190 metres (620 feet) above the town and 2285 metres (7500 feet) above sea level. The eight-minute ride in the glass-enclosed gondola gives you a magnificent view of the Bow Valley as you climb. At the top, you can enjoy the view from an observation deck or wander along the Vista Trail walkway to Sanson Peak. Canada's highest restaurant is the Panoramic Summit Restaurant. The tables are set against the windows, which are on a curve so that wherever you sit you will have a great view.

If you don't wish to take the gondola ride, sit on one of the benches on the edge of the parking lot and look out over the beautiful valley.

To see Bow Falls, turn right onto Spray Avenue when you reach the T on your way back along Mountain Avenue. Turn left at the Golf Course sign and then right onto Golf Course Road. Watch for the parking lot for Bow Falls. You can see the water churning

Bow Valley from Sulphur Mountain Gondola Lift

Bow Falls, Banff

over the steps carved in the rock. To your right, Spray River runs into the Bow River.

To reach the Banff Springs Hotel, go back to Spray Avenue and turn left. The Banff Springs Hotel was built by the CPR on the south bank of the Bow River in 1888. The CPR hoped the hotel would attract tourists to the area — tourists who would ride the railway to reach it.

Besides these popular attractions, there is a wide variety of sights to see and activities to do in Banff. The town has four museums and an

HOT SPRINGS

Hot springs do not originate from deep inside the Earth's core. They begin as run-off from rainfall or melting snow that drains down through interconnected faults to a depth of at least 2420 metres (7940 feet). Here the Earth's temperature is high enough to heat the water to the vaporizing point. As the water travels through the Earth, gases and chemicals dissolve in it and then either show up as deposits at the edge of the spring or as the rotten egg smell. As the steam rises through other faults, it cools and changes back into water. When it reaches the surface again, it is usually between 30°C (86°F) and 40°C (104°F).

Experiments done at Banff show that the water there takes about three months to complete its journey. At Yellowstone National Park, it takes 50 years.

Hoodoos near Banff

art gallery. The Banff Arts Festival lasts all summer. You could take a bus tour, or walk along Banff Avenue and visit the shops.

To see some of the sights outside of town, go north on Banff Avenue to Tunnel Mountain Road. Turn right and follow the narrow road through the chalets and resorts. In early June, elk may be spotted in the evenings among the trees at the no hook-up campsite. Some of the elk will be grazing, some will be lying down, and some will be watching you. Keep your pets on a leash and your children quiet and you will get some great pictures.

Past the campsite, watch for the sign for the hoodoos. There is a short trail from the parking lot to the viewpoint. If you want a better view, take the asphalt trail to two higher lookouts. The hoodoos, on top of the Bow embankment, were made by silt, rock and gravel bonded together by dissolved limestone. Over the centuries the loose ground around them has worn away, leaving these columns standing.

Back on the road only a kilometre (0.6 mile) from the hoodoos is the roadside turnout for Tunnel Mountain.

Tunnel Mountain is just a little mountain to the right of the viewpoint. An early survey map done for the CPR suggested building a tunnel under it. Although a route was eventually found around the

Cascade Falls

little mountain and there is no hole through it, it has carried the name Tunnel Mountain since 1882. Just across the road from the viewpoint is a campsite with full hook-ups.

Drive back to Banff Avenue, turn right, head towards the Trans-Canada Highway and cross it. Shortly afterwards you will come to the airport on your left and a sign for Cascade Pond on your right.

Cascade Pond is a nice little area for a picnic. In the centre of the pond is an island with wooden bridges out to it. There is a kitchen and picnic tables, but no camping is allowed. If you sit still, elk will munch contentedly on the grass while you watch.

Across the road from the Cascade Pond turn-off is a small parking area and the airport. Park in the lot and walk through the row of trees. Ahead you will see Cascade Falls plummeting down the side of the mountain. You can either take your pictures from here or walk across the open area to the beginning of the trail up to the base of the falls. The trail is steep and over loose rock. Going up is not bad, but coming down can be slippery.

Turn right onto the Johnson Lake road, which winds through the mountains and trees. Then turn left to bypass the turn-off to Johnson Lake in favour of Two Jack Lake, where you can launch your canoe on the lovely emerald-green waters.

Continue northwards to the Minnewanka day-use area; the road climbs and there are some viewpoints over Devil's Canyon and Lake Minnewanka. In 1912 a dam across Devil's Canyon raised the water of the lake by 4.8 metres (16 feet). A second dam in 1941 brought the water level up another 19.8 metres (65 feet), making the lake the largest in the park.

Lake Minnewanka and the Palliser Range

In addition to the day-use area at Lake Minnewanka there is a small marina. Here you can rent a boat or take a one-and-a-half hour cruise to see the foothills of Alberta through a gap in the mountains. Lake Minnewanka is the only body of water in Banff National Park where power boats are allowed. Anglers will want to try for Rocky Mountain whitefish, splake or lake trout, some of which weigh up to 13.6 kilograms (30 pounds). Scuba divers might want to check out the remains of the resort town of Minnewanka Landing preserved underwater off the point across the bay from the marina.

BANKHEAD

As you continue past Lake Minnewanka, looping back towards Banff, watch for the sign to Upper Bankhead and Cascade Valley. The ruins of the residential part of the Bankhead community are to the right of the cooking kitchen where the picnic tables are. Tall trees grow right out of the centre of the ruins. There are cement walls, some standing straight, some leaning and some fallen in.

Ore cars at Bankhead

Elk in the Park

If you want to see some of the mining operation, follow the path past the ruins. A sign warns you to stay on the path and watch for mine holes. This is the trail to C-Level Cirque, the highest level of the mines. It is 8 kilometres (5 miles) return and a fairly steep climb. Besides seeing ventilation shafts and old buildings, you will also be able to look down on Lake Minnewanka.

Just 0.5 kilometre (0.3 mile) further down the road from Upper Bankhead is Bankhead itself. At the parking lot is a viewpoint with a write-up about the town. To walk through the site, go down the steps leading from the lot. The buildings and ruins have interpretive signs near them explaining what had been there. A small engine with a line of coal cars behind sits on a track and inside the old transformer building is an exhibit of the mining era.

Bankhead was once a thriving coal mining town. In 1903, the CPR obtained a mining licence to begin mining the coal that had been discovered in 1883 along the edge of Cascade Mountain. The market was strong and all the coal produced in Bankhead was sold. At its height, it had a skating rink, tennis court, butcher shop, bakery and laundry. Twelve hundred people lived in the town, including 450 men who worked to take out 180,000 tonnes (200,000 tons) of coal each year.

However, a strike in 1912, falling markets and finally a general strike in 1922 brought about the end of the operation and the town. When the town died, most of the buildings were moved or demolished.

As you come out of the parking lot and turn left, there is a monument on the right put up in memory of eight men from here who died in the First World War. It is sheltered by a tall tree.

The road winds back down until you are at the Cascade Pond again. The whole tour takes about two hours depending on whether you decide to stop and have lunch.

MINING DIFFICULTIES

Although there was plenty of coal, mining in Cascade Mountain was difficult and costly. The coal seams were on a steep incline and tunnels had to be drilled higher and higher. The main coal tunnels ran for 55 kilometres (34 miles) and when added to the ventilation and transportation tunnels, the total length was more than 320 kilometres (200 miles).

The coal crumbled into dust as soon as it came to the top and in contact with the air, making it great for compressing with pitch into briquets for heating, but not good for use in train locomotives.

BOW VALLEY PARKWAY

Mountain sheep

If you are in a hurry to arrive in Kootenay National Park, take the Trans-Canada Highway to Highway 93 and turn southwards toward Radium. If you want a quieter, more scenic, slower drive, watch for a sign to the Bow Valley Parkway (Highway 1A). It is a narrow, winding road through the trees, with viewpoints, interpretive signs explaining the formation of the valley, mountain sheep and deer.

At kilometre 5.3 (mile 3.3) is the Muleshoe Picnic Area. Read the sign that explains how the hole in the mountain above was formed over the centuries by the water and glaciers.

Bow Valley Parkway

As you drive westwards along the Bow Valley Parkway, your lane is occasionally separated from the oncoming lane. At kilometre 12 (mile 7.5) the road divides but this time just around a tree. Story has it that when the highway was being built, the contractor liked this tree

Lower Falls, Johnston Canyon

so much that he refused to cut it down and the highway was built around it.

Five kilometres (3 miles) past that tree you reach Johnston Canyon with its two waterfalls. The hike to the first waterfall is 0.8 kilometres (0.5 mile); to the second, 2.4 kilometres (1.5 miles). Part of the trail to the lower falls is on catwalks that have been built along the canyon wall. Some sections are built right underneath the overhanging rock wall – if you are tall you will have to duck. Use the handrails if you want support as you walk. Once you have taken your pictures of the falls, you can crawl through a little tunnel where you can get a close-up, wet view of the water.

After the lower falls the trail sometimes leads away from the canyon, but you can still hear the roar of the water. There are no railings along the path so be careful. When you get close to the upper falls you will come to a Y. The trail to the right takes you down to the base of the falls in the canyon. The one on the left leads you higher up to the top of the falls. Both give you great pictures.

Back on the Bow Valley Parkway, you might want to read the sign at the site of the historic town of Silver City, 6 kilometres (3.7 miles) from Johnston Canyon. The town began in 1883 when silver, copper and lead were discovered in the area. Within

Upper Falls, Johnston Canyon

two years the ore ran out and Silver City disappeared. Stand and look out over the meadow and try to imagine a boom town with 2000 residents and 175 buildings here over a century ago.

Now turn around and you will have a great view of the back of Castle Mountain. (A better view is from Highway 93 in Kootenay National Park.) From Silver City, it is just a short drive to Castle Junction and the turn onto Highway 93, which leads into Kootenay National Park.

CASTLE MOUNTAIN

Castle Mountain was named by Sir James Hector of the Palliser Expedition in 1858. He was the first non-Native to view the mountain and its similarity to a castle led to its name.

After the Second World War, the residents of Scotland gave Dwight D. Eisenhower, General of the Allied Forces, a castle to show their appreciation. Prime Minister Mackenzie King, in an effort to top that, said that Canada would give Eisenhower an even larger castle and changed the name of Castle Mountain to Mount Eisenhower. Despite local protests the name remained until 1979.

In that year the original name was restored and the name Eisenhower Peak adorns the southernmost tower of the mountain. The treeless meadow below the tower is sometimes called Eisenhower's Putting Green.

KOOTENAY NATIONAL PARK

The Banff-Windermere Highway (Highway 93) runs the length of Kootenay National Park. Storm Mountain Lodge, at kilometre 4 (mile 2.5), is one of the oldest lodges in Banff National Park. It took its name from Storm Mountain, which usually has clouds around its summit.

Continental Divide

At the Continental Divide you are 1595 metres (5232 feet) above sea level. You are also on the boundary between British Columbia and Alberta and between Kootenay and Banff national parks. Behind the divide sign you can see where a stream divides, with part of the water flowing to the Columbia River and the Pacific Ocean, and part

Fireweed Trail

heading via the Bow, Saskatch-ewan and Nelson rivers to Hudson Bay.

In 1968 a fire burned over some 2300 hectares (6000 acres) of the park in just four days. While you are at the di-vide, take a walk on one of the Fireweed Trails to see some of the burn. The first trail takes about 10 minutes; the second goes higher and takes about 20 min-utes. Signs along the way explain what happened to the animals, birds, trees and plants. There are a lot of tall, grey spires that once were trees, but the new growth of lodgepole pines, trembling aspen and fir has come in so nicely that except for the dead trees still standing and the logs lying on the ground, you would hardly know there had been a fire.

Marble Canyon

Stop at Marble Canyon for a 1.5 kilometre (0.9 mile) self-guided walk along the side of the canyon and over seven bridges. Its name comes from the white marble throughout the area. The walls of the canyon are angular because the limestone and other rocks have been cracked into huge blocks by the heating and cooling effects of changing weather. Look down into the canyon and you will see the smooth hollows in the rock where the water rolled and twisted centuries ago. At the sev-enth bridge is a 21 metre (69 foot) waterfall.

Falls in Marble Canyon

The railings may seem a little too protective along some parts of the walk, but three people have fallen over the edge, two because they took one too many steps back when having their picture taken.

Old equipment at Paint Pots

An asphalt path 1.6 kilometres (1 mile) long leads to the Paint Pots. You follow the path and soon come to where the trail splits: one path is for wheelchairs and people who don't want such a steep descent. The paths meet again and you cross the Vermilion River on a suspension bridge. You walk beside the river, then through the trees to the ochre beds.

These ochre beds are a spillover area for waters that bubble up from the Earth. They are spread out over a large piece of ground and in the middle are small islands of grasses and trees. The water of the beds is clear and enhances the colour of the ground underneath. Wheelchairs can only go as far as these beds.

USNA'WAKI-CAGUBI

To the early Native peoples, the Paint Pots was a spiritual area and the home of the Red Clay Spirit. Their word 'usna'waki-cagubi' means 'where the red clay spirit is taken.' They made their own form of oil paint by taking the coloured clay and mixing it with water. They then kneaded it like bread and shaped it into flat cakes. These cakes were baked, then ground into powder and mixed with fish oil or animal grease to produce paint. This paint, which they used for painting rocks, has withstood centuries of weathering. Native peoples from as far away as the Great Plains came to gather the makings for colourful paints.

In the early 1900s, commercial mining of the beds began. Mining was stopped when Kootenay was named a national park in 1920. Some of the old machinery used in the mining lies rusting beside the path.

A paint pot forming

From the ochre beds you can follow Ruisseau Stream to the top of the hill, where you can see a new paint pot being formed. The stream bottom, the path you are on, and the hills around are all the same colour as the beds. The pots form around several active cold springs whose waters are full of dissolved iron. As the water bubbles up, the iron is deposited around the outlet. A mound grows around the spring until its the edge gets too high for the water to surmount; the underground liquid then seeks out a path of less resistance and begins a new pot. That pool of water with the mound around it is the new paint pot.

Numa Falls on the Vermilion River has a little picnic area. From the tables you can see the bridge and watch the water disappear over the edge of the falls. After lunch take the short walk to the bridge and see the face of the falls. You can take pictures from the bridge but it is hard to get all the falls in.

Vermilion River Crossing is 43 kilometres (26.7 miles) from the entrance to the park. On your left is Kootenay Park Lodge, with gas, camping, cabins and store. Past Vermilion River Crossing, the river, now on your left, is full of channels.

At the Simpson River parking area, the Simpson River flows into the Vermilion. You can leave your vehicle here and hike or ride a horse into Mount Assiniboine Provincial Park, a wilderness park. You can follow the Simpson River for 30 kilometres (18.6 miles) to a cabin along Surprise Creek. Trails lead from the cabin to Police Meadows, Mitchell Meadow and the park headquarters (near Lake Magog). Horses are allowed only in certain areas; obtain a permit from the district manager in the town of Wasa, to the south.

MOUNT ASSINIBOINE PROVINCIAL PARK

The area was used as a hunting ground by the Assiniboine for centuries before geologist G.M. Dawson arrived and named the highest peak Mount Assiniboine. At 3618 metres (11,870 feet) the mountain resembles the Matterhorn in Switzerland. In 1922, through the urging of the Alpine Club of Canada, the government of British Columbia designated 5120 hectares (12,650 acres) of land around the seventh-highest mountain in the Canadian Rockies as Mount Assiniboine Provincial Park. In 1973 the area was increased to 38,600 hectares (95,340 acres). In 1991 the park was designated a World Heritage Site by the United Nations.

Five peaks in this wilderness park reach 3100 metres (10,170 feet) or higher, and there is a wide variety of plants and wildlife and at least 93 different species of bird. Access is only by hiking or by horseback, or by helicopter on special days. Anyone considering mountain-climbing should be experienced.

Other approaches to Mount Assiniboine Provincial Park begin from Sunshine Meadows west of Banff, from Peter Lougheed Provincial Park in Alberta, and from Settlers Road.

Just after the Simpson River parking lot is a viewpoint with a monument to Sir George Simpson (1792-1860). Simpson was born in Scotland and joined the Hudson's Bay Company in 1820. One year later he was made governor of the northern department and in 1826 Governor-in-Chief of Rupert's Land.

Numa Falls

After you leave the monument, you drive down a hill and around a curve. There, you will see a sign on the left-hand side of the road stating 'animal lick.' If you are travelling through in the early morning or evening, watch for elk, moose and mule deer.

From the Hector Gorge viewpoint, you can see the Vermilion River flowing south to join the Kootenay River. Three kilometres (1.9 miles) from Hector Gorge, you come around a left-hand curve in the road. To the right on the edge of the trees is Kootenay Pond. There is a roadside turnout just ahead where you can park. Walk back to see the

Old equipment used to build the Banff-Windermere Highway

pond which, when the sun is shining, is a clear, transparent emerald green. Geologists believe the pond is a 'kettle' formed from a piece of ice that broke from a glacier and was buried under glacial sand and gravel. As the ice melted, the 'roof' fell in to form a depression.

Watch for the Kootenay Crossing viewpoint on the left. A sign here explains the building of the Banff-Windermere Highway and you can see some old equipment used in its construction. The road was built between 1910 and 1923 using horse-drawn slips and graders, which are much different than the equipment used today.

If you want to spend the night in Kootenay National Park, stop in at McLeod Meadows Campground. Watch for moose, elk and deer to come out and graze in the meadow at dusk. If you like a walk in the evening, take the 2.7 kilometre (1.7 mile) hiking trail from the interpretive centre in the campground to Dog Lake.

About 8 kilometres (5 miles) from McLeod Meadows Campground you will come to Settlers Road on the left. It is a winding, gravel road that (among other duties) provides access to Mount Assiniboine Provincial Park. At about kilometre 11 (mile 6.8) you leave Kootenay National Park and enter the Invermere Forest District. Here there is a split in the road. To the left is the Kootenay Palliser Forest Service Road and to the right is the Kootenay Settler Forest Service Road. Palliser River is to the left and Horseshoe Rapids are to the right.

The road to Horseshoe Rapids is narrow and winding. Watch for logging trucks, bear and deer. At kilometre 7 (mile 4.3) you come to a three-road split. Look to your right and you will see the Horseshoe Rapids. If you continue past the rapids, taking the centre road and keeping the Kootenay River to your left, you will eventually reach Canal flats on Highway 93/95 south of Radium.

Olive Lake

The Palliser Road will take you to the Nipika Touring Centre and the Palliser River.

Continuing along Highway 93 past Settlers Road, you come to a viewpoint overlooking the Kootenay River valley. There is a beautiful view of the valley down below with the river snaking through it, and another excellent view of the mountains on the other side overlapping each other. Interpretive signs tell about the red pine beetle and how it attacks the pine trees, killing them and turning their needles red.

KOOTENAY NATIONAL PARK

The eastern boundary of Kootenay National Park follows the Continental Divide, and its western border slopes down to the Rocky Mountain Trench. Because of the topography on its western side, there are differences in the weather, and hence the vegetation and animal life, between its north and south sections.

North along the Kootenay River to the McLeod Meadows the air is moist and the forest is subalpine with fir and Engelmann spruce. In the south the air is drier because it has left its rain or snow on the Purcell Mountains and has swept across the Rocky Mountain Trench. Here the forest is patchy and consists of dry Douglas-fir.

The park has 200 kilometres (125 miles) of hiking trails on which you can see bighorn sheep, mountain goats, moose, bears and many smaller animals. Birds include the golden eagle, red crossbill, gray jay and white-tailed ptarmigan.

At Olive Lake, you are at Sinclair Pass Summit, which has an altitude of 1486 metres (4875 feet). You can picnic beneath the towering pines and spruce. From the parking lot a trail leads to the right and to a Y in the path. The trail to the right goes to the edge of the lake where you can watch little fish swimming near the shore.

The path to the left takes you to a bridge over a stream that is an outlet for the lake. From the bridge you follow a gravel pathway to a boardwalk. At the end of the boardwalk you can see the stream that bubbles into the lake. This stream flows year-round and does not freeze in the winter.

Olive Lake, a stopping site for native hunting groups, gets its name from the olive hue of the waters. The signs along the pathways tell about the bears, trees and people who first came here. One such group was made up of Red River emigrants who, led by a Metis named James Sinclair, crossed Sinclair Pass in 1841, went down Sinclair Canyon to the Columbia River Valley, and finally settled in the Oregon Territory.

Sinclair Canyon

When you leave Olive Lake, the highway passes by it and you can see just how small it is. As you drive west you will be travelling alongside the Sinclair River.

Sinclair Canyon, on the plane of a major fracture called the Redwall Fault, is amazing with its tall, red walls. This rusty red colour comes from the oxidation of the iron in the rock. The red walls gradually narrow and you reach the Iron Gates Tunnel. This tunnel was cut through the limestone and dolomite rock and it is a short but fun drive.

Then you reach one of the parking lots for the Radium Hot Springs Aquacourt on the left side of the road. Just across the road is the best view of the canyon walls. From here it is a 300 metre (985 foot) stroll through tall, shaded trees and beside Sinclair Creek to the hot springs pools. Lights are spaced so that the area is well lit in the evening. If you don't want to walk, drive a little further to the parking lot on the other side of the springs.

Iron Gates Tunnel

There are two pools, the hot pool at 39°C (102°F) and the cool at 29°C (84°F). Before your soak in the pools you might want to try a massage. Afterwards, you might want to take in the displays showing the history of the springs. There is also a restaurant if you are hungry.

Radium Hot Springs

The waters of Radium Hot Springs do not have the rotten egg smell of other hot springs. Although they have a lower mineral content than other springs in the Rockies, they are high in calcium from the surrounding rock and contain dissolved sodium, potassium, magnesium and other minerals. On the day after the Alaska earthquake in 1964, the waters of the spring had a definite reddish-brown colouration. It is believed that minor movements in the Redwall Fault caused small amounts of the oxidized iron to be released into the hot springs.

For centuries the hot springs were kept secret by the Kutenai people. In 1841 Sir George Simpson was made aware of them. They were purchased in 1890 by Englishman Roland Stuart for $160. The first road through the Continental Divide was built and soon the rich, the adventurous and the sick were flocking here. When Kootenay National Park was formed, the springs were expropriated at the cost of $40,000 so they could be included in the park.

Sinclair Canyon

Just before you leave the park you drive through the narrowest part of the canyon. The walls are so close to your vehicle you can almost reach out and touch them. When you come out of them drive around the curve ahead to the parking lot for the viewpoint.

From the viewpoint you can see out over the valley, take pictures of the falls created by the creek, or walk on the sidewalk back through that narrow canyon. It is absolutely lovely here.

As you leave Kootenay National Park you drive downhill with a gorgeous view of the valley below.

CHAPTER 3
GOLDEN TO FORT STEELE

Orchard planted over 100 years ago in the Wild Horse area

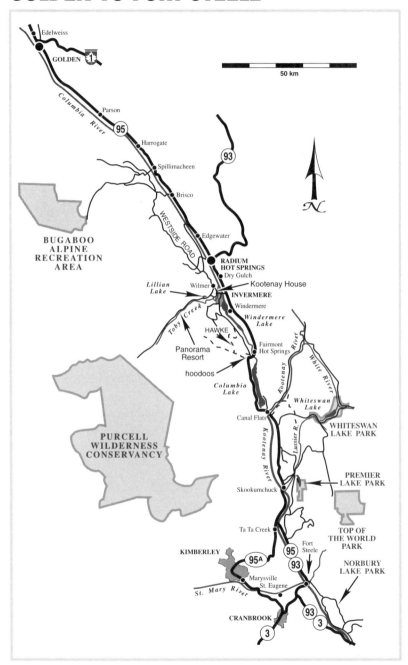

In a province of mountain roads, this highway is the straightest and most level of them all. The reason is that it travels through the Rocky Mountain Trench. The trench is a major geological fault line that runs for 1500 kilometres (930 miles) north and south along the western side of the Rocky Mountains. All the way south the Rockies will be to the left and the Purcells to the right.

GOLDEN TO RADIUM

GOLDEN

In Golden you can stand in the centre of town, turn all around, and everywhere you stop you will see mountains.

Golden was first called Golden City by the railway men in an effort to outdo Silver City down the line near Banff. It started out as a ragged bunch of tents in 1883 and as cabins, stores and numerous saloons were added, it became a rip-roaring town. When the construction of the tracks was finished, unlike most towns which quickly died, Golden grew and prospered, mainly because it was at the confluence of the Columbia and Kicking Horse rivers. In 1896 the 'City' was dropped from its name.

By the 1890s, mountain climbing in the area was such a popular sport that the CPR began bringing in Swiss guides to take tourists on climbing expeditions. In 1911 the village of Edelweiss was built by the CPR to accommodate the guides and decrease their need to return home at the end of each summer. The last of the original guides died in 1981 at the age of 96; his granddaughter now owns and rents out five of the six chalets of Edelweiss. The sixth one was the one she was raised in.

If you want to watch some hang-gliding, take Highway 1 towards Field and turn left at the Golden-Donald Upper Road. On

Reflection Lake south of Golden

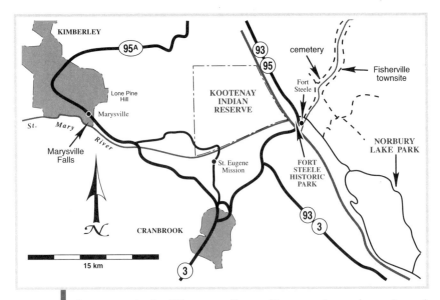

KIMBERLEY

95A

Lone Pine
Hill

Marysville

St. Mary River

Marysville
Falls

KOOTENAY
INDIAN
RESERVE

St. Eugene
Mission

93
95

cemetery

Fort
Steele

Fisherville
townsite

NORBURY
LAKE PARK

FORT
STEELE
HISTORIC
PARK

93
3

N

CRANBROOK

15 km

3

the corner is the Discovery Centre. You can sit on the patio and watch the hang-gliders take off from the gliding platform on Mount Seven to the south. There is a radio hook-up with the gliders so you can listen to their conversations. The centre opened in 1994 and has displays and videos about the Rocky Mountain Trench, the Columbia Valley and the Burgess Shale fossils. Mount Seven is renowned for its exceptional thermal updrafts.

The Golden and District Museum is at the southern end of Golden. Turn left off 10th Avenue onto 12th Street and then take the first right. The museum has a variety of displays, one of which is a complete collection of the town's newspaper, the Golden *Star*, dating back to 1891.

COLUMBIA VALLEY WETLANDS

The Columbia Valley has been called the 'Serengeti' of North America. From Reflection Lake near Golden south to Brisco are a number of sloughs with lily pads floating on them. These sloughs, part of the Columbia Valley Wetlands, are a favourite haven for wildlife in the area.

Many animals including cougars, timber wolves, elk and moose inhabit the area and over 200 bird species have been recorded. Conservationists agree that this is one of the last great wetlands in Canada and possibly the world.

Just 1 kilometre (0.6 mile) south of Golden is the Reflection Lake Wildlife Viewing Area. Turn to your left after the sign and follow the road in. The marsh is to your right and you will come to a viewing stand (or 'blind'). The blind was developed by the Golden branch of the East Kootenay Environmental Society using volunteer labour and the generous contributions of other businesses. There is a telescope for you to look out over the lake at the birds swimming and nesting. Some birds you might see are marsh wrens, ruddy ducks, great blue herons, cinnamon teals, coots, ospreys and common goldeneyes. Also watch for muskrats, water striders and cattails.

NICHOLSON TO EDGEWATER

As you head south, to the west is the Columbia River meandering northwards along the bottom of the Rocky Mountain Trench. flyfishers will want to try for rainbow trout up to 5 kilograms (11 pounds). Walleye up to 3 kilograms (6.6 pounds) are also found in this river.

RIVER GRADES

Rivers are graded as to their difficulty. Grade I is easy, with no natural obstructions, such as rocks. Grade II has fairly frequent rapids. As the rapids become more difficult, the water is upgraded to Grade III. Grade IV has long stretches of difficult rapids. Grade V has continuous violent rapids, fast current and obstructions. It should be scouted first and open canoes must portage. Grade VI is termed unnavigable. It is very dangerous and should be portaged.

Log carvings by the Radium Carver

With the exception of Edgewater, the hamlets along this section of road are small: a store, a gas station and a few residences. From any of them you can put a canoe in the Columbia River and paddle through the wetlands. If you want a very long trip, put your canoe in at Fairmont Hot Springs and take it out at Donald Station north of Golden. While travelling through the marshes, watch for blue herons, eagles, swans and ospreys and animals coming down to the shore to drink from the waters. This is a Grade I river and is good for novices, families or anyone who likes a quiet trip through a river habitat.

Spillimacheen and Brisco both have road access to Bugaboo Glacier Provincial Park. This wilderness hiking park is in the most northern part of the Purcell Mountains, which rose up over 1500 million years ago. At that time, the only lifeform was algae. Since the Palliser Expedition trekked over these mountains in 1857-60, loggers, fur traders, miners and mountain climbers have come to the area. Bugaboo Glacier Provincial Park and Bugaboo Alpine Recreation Area were designated in 1969; the park has 358 hectares (884 acres) and the recreation area has 24,624 hectares (60,845 acres). Bugaboo Glacier Provincial Park has the largest icefields of the Purcells within its borders.

Carvings by the Radium Carver

Remember that it is a wilderness park with no supplies, so if you decide to visit you have to bring all your own equipment. The weather changes quickly and hail, lightning or snowstorms can suddenly appear.

If you are in the area on a Saturday watch for the signs to the Edgewater Open Market. The market has operated since 1971 and offers produce, crafts, baked goods, jams, woodworking and much more. Vegetable-growing has been part of the Edgewater area since its beginning before the First World War, when a community irrigation system was set up to water the surrounding fields. This irrigation resulted in the town being able to send two truckloads of produce a week to the hotels in Jasper and Banff during the Depression.

RADIUM

Windermere Valley

Radium is at the junction of Highways 95 and 93. It is just southwest of Radium Hot Springs in Kootenay National Park.

At the four-way stop, turn to your left onto Highway 93 north. In less than a block is Madsen Road – turn right onto Madsen and drive up to the entrance to the Radium Carver's shop. You will recognize the shop by the fence of huge, upright logs. Inside the building are clocks, carvings of people, mirrors, vases and more. Outside in the yard are larger, more light-hearted work, including a pink lookout tower, effigies hanging from poles, geese wandering around, and carvings of animals and people. All the carver's work is for sale and he has a worldwide market.

Don't be surprised by the Radium Carver's long, dyed hair and his mad-trapper look. He is a very interesting person to talk with. He was born in Switzerland and has been doing his craft in Radium since 1976.

Radium Days is celebrated on the weekend following Victoria Day and the Annual Columbia Classic Car Show is held in September.

You are just barely out of Radium when you come to a series of four viewpoints overlooking the valley. Any one of them gives a magnificent view.

At the town of Dry Gulch, take your children to drive the go-carts at Nascarts, or take them to Playland, which has a miniature golf course and playground. Two kilometres (1.2 miles) down the highway is the Log Cabin Antiques store. The room is heated by an old wood stove and the lights hang from wagon wheels.

INVERMERE TO SKOOKUMCHUCK

INVERMERE

Miner's cabin in Windermere Valley

You are travelling along the edge of the Windermere Valley. Across the valley are huge golden cliffs. Turn off the highway and make a winding downhill descent into Invermere. On the way you have a great view of Windermere Lake, formed by a widening in the Columbia River, on your left. Just as you get to the top of the hill into the town, you will see the Windermere Valley Museum on the right-hand side. There is the old Brisco schoolhouse, a prospector's cabin and a railway station. Each building is furnished with artifacts from the era it was used. In the museum is a copy of the journal of David Thompson. From the museum you can look out over the valley and the lake.

If you wish to see a variety of artists and their work, visit the Treetop Artwalk from mid-July to mid-August. Drive west through town until you reach 13th Avenue and turn south; 13th Avenue eventually becomes Westside Road. Watch for Johnson Road about 1.6 kilometres (1 mile) out of town. The Treetop Artwalk is on the northwest corner of these two roads.

The artwalk is the idea of Christine and Trevor Wignall. Artisans from British Columbia and Alberta set their work up on the Wignalls' 1.6 hectares (4 acres) of land. You will see stained glass designs hanging from trees, pottery, jewellery, metalwork and wood-carvings. Just walking around the summer woods and seeing the Rocky Mountains is worth the visit. The Wignalls began their artwalk in 1994 with one week of displays, and the response was so good that they have expanded it to one month.

On your way out of Invermere past the museum, take the first turn left onto the road to Wilmer and Panorama Resort. The road winds through the industrial part of town. On the edge of town you cross a bridge over Toby Creek and come to a T intersection. This road is the Toby Creek Road: to the right is Wilmer, to the left Panorama Resort.

WILMER AND PANORAMA

Delphine Lodge at Wilmer

Take the road to Wilmer. Half a kilometre (0.6 mile) from the bridge is the Kootenae House David Thompson historic site. It is a fenced area with a monument in the centre. David Thompson built a fort here in 1807 and used it as a base for his explorations of the Kootenay and Columbia rivers. In 1812 clashes with the Peigans forced the post to close.

Along the road to Wilmer, you drive beside the golden cliffs you saw from across the valley. In Wilmer just continue on the road until you come to the end of the pavement at Main Avenue. Turn right and go two blocks to the blue-sided Delphine Lodge. Originally known as the Delphine Hotel, it was built in 1899. It has since been turned into a lodge.

If you want some beautiful views of Invermere, Windermere Lake, the valley and mountains, go back to the bridge and take the road up to Panorama Resort. Along the way you pass olive-green Lillian Lake, which has a recreational area. The road follows a creek for much of the distance.

Panorama Resort is not just a winter resort. It has tennis courts, trail rides, wild water rafting and guided hikes through the wilderness. If you are there in late August, you can take in the Annual Scottish gathering hosted by the resort.

WINDERMERE

Windermere is off the highway and is an artists' haven. During the summer, an artists' market is held in the centre of the village.

Two buildings to visit are the Stolen Church and the White House Pub. Both were built in Donald 140 kilometres (87 miles) to the north. Soon after Celina Kimpton moved from Donald, she began to wish for the church she had attended in that village. Her husband, Rufus, went to Donald with some friends, dismantled the church and rebuilt it in Windermere. It is now called the Stolen Church and is open to visitors. Later they also moved the White House from Donald and operated it as a pub.

Hoodoos near Fairmont Hot Springs

To find the Stolen Church, turn off Highway 93/95 onto Windermere Road. Follow it to Sinclair Avenue. The Community Hall is on your left. Across Sinclair Avenue is the church. To get to the White House Pub, turn left on Sinclair and it is about a block down the street.

The climate and topography in the Windermere area is quite diverse. There are moist and dry lands and low and high elevations, and because of this variation there is a wide variety of plant life. Most of this area is in the Rocky Mountain Trench, and wilderness mountain parks include Mount Assiniboine, Top of the World and Bugaboo Glacier.

FAIRMONT HOT SPRINGS AND CANAL FLATS

Baths at Fairmont Hot Springs

Fairmont's odourless Hot Springs Pools are the largest in Canada. If you don't want to go to the hot springs, park in the lot and climb the hill across the road to the 'Indian Baths' used by the Kutenai people for centuries. You can sit on the benches and look out over the valley.

One kilometre (0.6 mile) from Fairmont are the hoodoos, which you can see from the road. Across the road is a resort where you can get ice cream, gas and supplies.

The Westside Road begins beside the hoodoos and is a backroad into Invermere. It is old pavement with pot-holes. If you like to four-wheel drive, follow Hawke Road up into hills to the power line for some four-wheeling.

South of Columbia Lake you are into the flats – low marshy land with ponds of water. Look for the remains of the Baillie-Grohman Canal. This canal was built in the 1880s to connect Columbia Lake with the Kootenay River, which flows south. W.A. Baillie-Grohman was an Englishman who, hoping to reclaim the land, built a canal with one lock to join the two waterways. The canal was eventually shut down with only two steamboats, the *Gwendoline* in 1894 and the *Northstar* in 1902, having passed through its lock. Many feared that it might raise the water level of the Columbia River and flood the transcontinental railway track near Golden.

Columbia Lake

The hamlet of Canal Flats has an avenue named after Baillie-Grohman.

For some rugged mountain driving, turn onto the road to White-swan Lake Provincial Park 6 kilometres (3.7 miles) south of Canal Flats. It is narrow, gravel, hilly, full of curves and pot-holes, and has some sheer drop-offs. You also have to watch for logging trucks, but the scenery is great as you follow the White River.

At kilometre 16.7 (mile 10.4) you come to the entrance to the park. Pull into the parking area and walk to the little covered deck. There are some steps and then a steep descent down a path to the Lussier Hot Springs. The pool is about the size of an 8–12-person hot tub. You can either sit in the water or on a bench built over one end and dangle your feet. The pool is right beside the Lussier River and it is very relaxing to sit there and watch the river flow by.

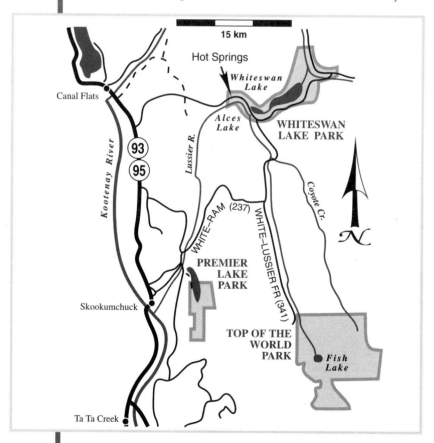

Lussier Hot Springs

About 4 kilometres (2.5 miles) later you actually reach Moose (Alces) Lake Campground. This campground is very popular so get there early. Motorboats are prohibited on Alces Lake and fishing is restricted to fly-fishing. Birdwatchers should watch for the bald and golden eagles that make the park their home year-round.

When you reach the campground you will come to a Y intersection. Turn left to go into the campground, or turn right if you wish to continue on to Top of the World Provincial Park.

The road to Top of the World is called the White-Lussier Forest Service Road. You immediately begin to climb as soon as you get on it. At kilometre 5 (mile 3.1), you come to the Ram Creek burn area. Lightning started a fire here in 1985, which burned 13,000 hectares (32,000 acres).

The road descends into a valley. From the valley floor you can look up the mountainside and see the stark, grey, dead trees rising above the green of the new forest.

At kilometre 15.8 (mile 9.8) you come to a crossroads with the White-Ram Forest Service Road. According to the government Forest Recreation map, you are on #341 and the White-Ram road is #237. If you are running out of time, turn right on #237 and follow it west to Highway 93/95 at Skookumchuck (travel on this backroad is described below). To reach the Top of the World just carry on straight ahead.

Fish ladder at Premier Lake Provincial Park

Four kilometres (2.5 miles) from the crossroads you leave the burn area and the mountains around you are green again. It looks and feels good to be back among the green trees again.

The entrance to Top of the World is 30.5 kilometres (19 miles) from Whiteswan. It is a wilderness park accessible only by hiking or by horseback riding in some areas. A sign gives you trail information and describes wilderness ethics and being prepared for hiking in the back country.

Horses are allowed on the Coyote Creek, Galbraith Creek and Fish Lake trails only. At Fish Lake the horses must be kept away from the cabin and they are permitted to graze overnight only at the Coyote Creek Cabin, Sayles Meadows and Nicole Creek campground.

TOP OF THE WORLD

Top of the World Provincial Park gets its name from being high in the Kootenay Ranges of the Rocky Mountains. Most of the park is above 1800 metres (5900 feet). Mount Morro, the highest peak in the park, has an elevation of 2912 metres (9554 feet).

Native peoples came from the Shuswap and Montana to obtain chert, a grey, translucent, obsidian-like rock, to make tools and weapons. There are many archaeological sites in the park.

Birdwatchers should watch for scaups and buffleheads, which rest here on their migrations. Birds that stay during the summer are spotted sandpipers, Steller's jays, whiskey-jacks, Clark's nutcrackers and white-winged crossbills.

On your way back, when you reach the crossroads turn west onto the White-Ram Forest Service Road (#237) and it will take you back to Highway 93/95. For a truly backroad wilderness experience, this is the road. At one point it is just barely wide enough for one vehicle and has a drop-off into a canyon below. A little further on, part of the roadside has fallen away so that you lose what little shoulder you might have had.

Premier Lake

Then at kilometre 16.4 (mile 10.2) the wilderness experience is over and you are on pavement again. When you reach the Y, take the left fork to continue on to Highway 93/95. If, however, you are looking for a place to relax after your trip through the back country, watch for the sign for Premier Lake Provincial Park at kilometre 1.6 (mile 1). You turn left onto the road to the park. Three kilometres (1.9 miles) down the road you enter the Premier Lake Provincial Park. There are picnic areas, a campground and a boat launch.

If you are camping in late May or June, go down the path along Staple Creek and watch the trout work their way upstream to spawn. They are a dark brown, almost the same colour as the rocks in the water, but they are long and show up easily. As you walk beside the creek you can hear them splash as they try to leap over obstructions in their path.

It is a nice trail and takes you right out to the lake. You can see where a ladder has been built to make it easier for the fish to work their way up from the lake to the creek. Trout eggs are taken from the fish in this lake for the hatchery near Wardner.

Anglers can try for the 'Gerrard Giants,' also known as the Gerrard rainbow trout, in any of the four lakes in the park.

Pulp plant near Skookumchuck

To reach Highway 93/95, go back to the paved road and turn left. At kilometre 7.3 (mile 4.5) is a split in the road. Take the left-hand split and you will reach the highway. The terrible smell is from the pulp plant that is less than a kilometre (half a mile) south along the highway. You can stop in at the roadside turnout for a view of the Kootenay River, the valley and the pulp plant.

Skookumchuck has a service station, store and camping. The name sounds funny in English but it is a Native word meaning 'turbulent' or 'rapid torrent,' signifying what the Kootenay River must have been like at one time in this area.

KIMBERLEY TO FORT STEELE

KIMBERLEY

World's largest clock, Kimberley

Thirty-six kilometres (22.4 miles) south of Skookumchuck you come to the junction in the highway. Ahead on Highway 95A is Kimberley, which turned 100 in 1996. To the left is Fort Steele.

The Platzl of Kimberley comprises two streets that have been blocked off to vehicle traffic by planters across the road. The red-brick, tree-lined walkway has a few houses along it, but there are mainly shops with their fronts renovated in the Bavarian style. There is a little fountain, a creek with arched bridges, and a centre bandstand. On the hour, Happy Hans, the town's mascot, pops out of the world's largest clock and yodels a song. If you miss that, you can put a quarter in a slot on the right side and Happy Hans will come out and yodel his song for you.

It is easy to believe that you have been transported to a town in Austria or Bavaria. You smell the food, are waited on by servers in dirndls and lederhosen, sit outside at umbrella-covered tables, and see all the painted shops and hanging baskets. But then you see the signs for Stedmans, Mcleods and Radio Shack, and you are suddenly brought back to reality. However, the scenery here is just as wonderful as it is in the Alps.

From the Platzl, take Gerry Sorensen Way (Sorenson, a Kimberley native, was the 1982 winner of the Ladies' Downhill Ski Championship) and follow it past the walls of reddish-orange rock that have been exposed by the Cominco Sullivan Mine. This mine is

The Platzl, Kimberley

the largest silver, lead and zinc producer in the world. It began operation as the Sullivan Mine in the early 1890s and was bought by Cominco in 1909. It is scheduled to close in 2001.

Further up, where Gerry Sorensen Way meets Norton Avenue, you come to the Old Bauernhaus on the left. The 41 tonne (45 ton) timber building was constructed in southern Bavaria in 1640 and has had many uses since then. When the present owners, Tony and Ingrid Schwarzenberger, decided they wanted to move to Kimberley, they dismantled the family home and brought it with them. Rebuilding was completed in 1989 and the home is now a restaurant that serves tasty Bavarian food. If you are a non-smoker you will be seated where cows, working horses and pigs were once kept. Smokers have the pleasure of knowing that at one time the bench they are sitting on held caged chickens beneath it.

To reach the Happy Hans Campground, continue on Gerry Sorensen Way until you see the railway station on your right. If you camp here for the night, you can play miniature golf, browse through the gift shop or take a trip on the Bavarian City Mining Railway. The railway was opened in 1984 with a 2.5 kilometre (1.6 mile) loop that begins at the campground, takes you past the Sullivan Mine, over a 61 metre (200 foot) long, 7.6 metre (25 foot) high trestle, on a riding tour through the mining museum, and down into the bushlands. In 1996 the tour was expanded to include downtown Kimberley.

If you are in Kimberley in early July, take in the annual six-day accordion festival. The festival began in 1974 and is the only old-time accordion competition in

Happy Hans, Kimberley

Bavarian City Mining Railway Station

North America. It brings guest artists from around the world for your enjoyment, and competitors try for the thousands of dollars in prize money. Impromptu jam sessions are held at the Platzl throughout the week.

A walk through the Cominco Gardens is a perfect way to end the day. From the set of lights on Highway 95A, turn right and follow the hospital signs to the hospital. Drive one block past the entrance and turn left. It is only a block from there. Watch for the signs. The 1 hectare (2.5 acre) gardens were begun in 1927 to promote Cominco's Elephant Brand fertilizer. When the gardens were transferred to the town, the stipulation was made that they keep their original name. Besides shrubs and perennials, 10,000 bedding plants are set out each year. Enjoy a stroll along the wheelchair-accessible paths and smell the fragrant flowers. Admission is by donation.

MARYSVILLE AND ST. EUGENE CHURCH

Mark Creek runs through the town of Kimberley to Marysville. To see Marysville Falls, as soon as you cross the bridge over the creek in Marysville turn left into the parking lot. From the lot you cross the street to the Al Fabro/ Mark Creek walk. You cross the creek on a bridge and follow a boardwalk alongside it. You pass three cascades, then the boardwalk ends and a pathway takes you through the trees. The canyon suddenly and quickly deepens, and a fence has been built to prevent anyone from wandering too close to the edge.

When you reach the falls, you can take your pictures from the lookout point. The path continues past the falls if you wish to go further.

Marysville Falls

The Rocky Mountain Chocolate Factory is on the corner just a block from the parking lot. It boasts of having the largest selection of handmade chocolates in the East Kootenays. If you like chocolate, you had better stop in and try the homemade fudge, truffles or Italian ice cream. People worried about calories will be happy to know that the factory makes sugar-free chocolates.

The road to St. Eugene Church is 18.5 kilometres (11.5 miles) from Marysville. The church is on the St Mary's Indian Band Reserve and was built using the money from two mining claims that a Kutenai person named Pierre had discovered. It is the white building with red alcoves around the windows on the right side of the road. The church was restored in 1983 and if you wish to see inside you have to ask permission.

That large, old stone building with the faded roof across the road from the church is the old reservation schoolhouse. It was built in 1912, and Native children from the Kootenays and the Okanagan were housed and taught there. It is the largest surviving heritage building in the area.

FORT STEELE

Continue south on Highway 95A, then turn left on Highway 3/95 towards Fort Steele. The first historic object you will see is a huge paddle wheel set up on a hill. Drive past that and take the left-hand turn off the highway. In the parking lot are rows of tall trees with picnic tables under them. You can have your lunch before or after visiting the park.

A map of the site is available at the entrance. It identifies the various buildings. There are over 60, with 52 of them being original or reconstructions of the original buildings.

Some of the businesses are operated as they were at the end of the last century. The bakery has an oven large enough to bake dozens

Reconstructed North-West
Mounted Police Post, Fort Steele

Perry Creek waterwheel, Fort Steele

of loaves. Stop here for a cup of coffee and a cinnamon bun. Mrs. Sprague's Confectionery and the General Store are both open for business.

You can walk down the restored frontier main street and stop for tea and home baking at the replica of the Wasa Hotel, which is also the museum. Or you can take in a first-class, live, musical comedy stage show at the Wildhorse Theatre, British Columbia's largest indoor summer theatre. You can watch an old printing press in action, see a blacksmith working over a forge, or watch a quilt being made. You can ride on a stagecoach or on the Dunromin train.

Many of the residents are volunteers who dress in period costumes and discuss the events in the area – the events of the late 1880s that is.

A NAME CHANGE

After the gold rush ended, settlers moved in and began cattle ranching and farming, causing the Upper Kutenai people much concern over their land. In 1887, Sam Steele and 75 North-West Mounted Policemen went to Galbraith's Ferry to quell the dispute over land ownership. The problem was settled without a shot being fired and the force left in 1888. To honour the man for his achievement, Galbraith's Ferry changed its name to Fort Steele.

The town boomed during the next decade owing to silver-lead discoveries in the East Kootenays, but when the railway picked Cranbrook as its stopping point in 1897, the population of the town dropped from 3000 to 200. In 1961 the Fort Steele Heritage Park was established and restoration began.

When you leave Fort Steele turn left onto the highway and then immediately turn right onto the road to Norbury Provincial Park. A campsite is at the corner there, or you can drive further to Norbury Provincial Park.

About a kilometre (half a mile) down the road you will come to the Fort Steele-Wild Horse Road, a gravel road to the left. You have to watch for this road, as it branches off at the top of a hill and the sign is hidden by bushes. Turn left and to make sure you have the right road, drive past the first clump of trees to the orange and white painted power poles. On the top of one of the poles is currently an osprey nest.

The road is gravel and winding. It is a single lane with occasional pullouts. At kilometre 5 (mile 3) you will see a sign that says 'Historical Trails' and the road makes a sharp, hairpin right and begins to climb steeply. In less than a kilometre (0.6 mile), look down below the road to the right and you will see a white roof over a map, and a cemetery full of white crosses. A vehicle trail goes down the hillside to the map. Drive down – the map shows you where you can park further on. The parking lot itself is just a clearing in the trees that will hold about three vehicles. You can walk from here on the last 1.6 kilometres (1 mile) of the Dewdney Trail. There are many historical sites along the way marked by signs.

The first gold rush in the East Kootenays took place in 1864 on a creek called Stud Horse. The prospectors had seen a wild stallion in the area and christened the rich creek after it. The town of Fisherville immediately sprang up on the site and was named after one of the miners. It had a population of over 5000, six general stores, two butcher shops, a blacksmith and four saloons at the end of its first year.

In 1865 Stud Horse Creek paid better than any California creek during its heyday. It yielded the Fisher Company of six partners $100,000 in gold (1865 dollars), the Dore Company of 10 partners about $150,000, Reese and Company about $76,000, Griffith and Company of three partners $30,000. Others also took out thousands but much of that went south of the border.

Fisherville Cemetery

Then someone discovered that a rich vein ran under the town. The buildings of Fisherville were quickly moved or demolished. Those that were moved higher up the hill formed the town of Wild Horse, the name Stud Horse Creek having been changed to Wild Horse Creek by a government official who thought the original name inappropriate.

DEWDNEY TRAIL

Because it was easier and shorter to travel north to Fisherville by way of the Kootenay River than to struggle overland from New Westminster, the population of Fisherville consisted mainly of Americans. Their supplies came from south of the border and they took their gold back with them when they left. To stem this outflow, the BC government ordered the construction of an extension to the Dewdney Trail from Rock Creek to Fisherville. This trail had been completed from Hope to Rock Creek under the direction of Edgar Dewdney in 1859.

Edgar Dewdney was again put in charge and given one year to complete the 1.2 metre (4 foot) wide, 645 kilometre (400 mile) long trail over three mountain ranges. He completed the trail in 1865, but by then the gold boom in Fisherville was over. Much later, his trail was used as the basis for 80% of today's Highway 3 route.

One of the historical sites along this part of the trail is the grave of Thomas Walker. It is slightly more than a quarter kilometre (a sixth of a mile) from the road, and signs describe some of his history. He was born in Donegal, Ireland and died of wounds from a gunfight with 'Yeast Powder' Bill on August 6, 1864.

The grave is straight downhill and has a replica of the original headboard inside a windowed case. A few years ago, a couple named Egge from Fort Steele took the original headboard home and kept it at the proper temperature. After two years, Mrs. Egge was able to retrace the original lettering on the board. The board was brought back here and set in the case, which was made by the Historical Association of the East Kootenays. But fear of vandalism and deterioration made them remove the original and replace it with this replica. The original is at the museum at Fort Steele.

Walker grave and replica of headboard

The trail also takes you to the first orchard in the East Kootenays, planted in 1872 by Dave Griffith. Some of the original trees are now over 100 years old. The trees were brought 725 kilometres (450 miles) on horseback over summits and across streams to this site.

CHAPTER 4

CROWSNEST PASS TO CRESTON

Rail car at Canadian Museum of Rail Travel in Cranbrook

CROWSNEST PASS TO CRESTON

This road is full of the name Moyie. There is Moyie Lake, Moyie River, Moyie Mountain Range, the town of Moyie, Moyie Lake Provincial Park. These 'Moyie's are all in a section of BC around Cranbrook and Creston. As you drive this section, perhaps you can figure out what 'Moyie' means.

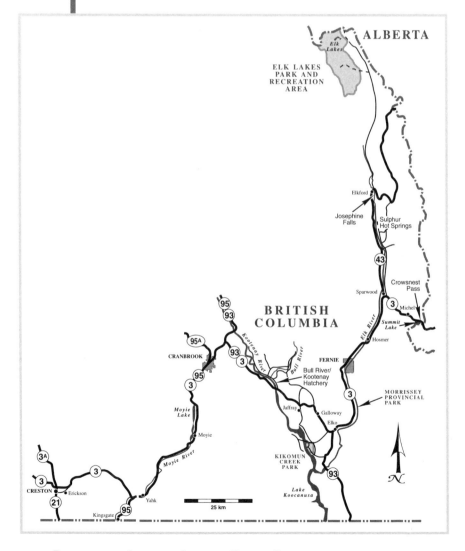

CROWSNEST PASS TO FERNIE

THE BORDER

At the Alberta-British Columbia border on Highway 3, you cross the Continental Divide at an altitude of 1396 metres (4580 feet). As you enter British Columbia, watch for the sign for the Inn on the Border. To reach the inn, make a sharp left turn down a hill off the highway. The inn is a tall building over 75 years old. It used to be a bar but now it has a restaurant, hot tubs and a bed-and-breakfast.

If you wish to fish in Summit Lake you have to take the road down past the Inn on the Border. At the lake there is a two fish daily limit and 30 cm (11.8 inch) minimum size. Rainbow trout up to 5.4 kilograms (12 pounds) have been caught in this lake.

MICHEL

At kilometre 13.7 (mile 8.5) you come to the Michel Hotel and Pub, the only building left of the once-thriving town of Michel. Just past the hotel are some old brick buildings, one with '1908' on it, that are the remains of the mining industry.

Michel, named after Chief Michel of the Kutenai, was established in 1897. When the railway went through, miners and their families settled here. Ten years later, another village was founded. First it was called New Michel, then Natal. Within a few years other communities – Middleton, Little Chicago, 'Up the Valley' (the Elk Valley) and later Sparwood – joined Michel and Natal. But tragedy was never far away in these mining towns.

Michel was almost destroyed by fire in 1902. Mine disasters took their toll in 1904, 1916, 1938 and 1967. Although the residents were a close-knit group who survived severe winters, flood and accidents, these communities disappeared in the late 1960s, when the BC government decided the southwestern entrance into the province needed enhancing and so moved the people to Sparwood and burned the buildings.

Two kilometres (1.2 miles) from the Michel Hotel and Pub, you come to a little park on your right. A plaque tells the story of Michel and Natal. Watch for a herd of elk that frequently grazes in the area.

Sulphur Hot Springs pool near Elkford

To reach Elkford, watch for the sign along Highway 3 as you enter Sparwood, and turn north onto Highway 43. You are now in the Elk Valley. For the first couple of kilometres (1 to 2 miles) across the valley on your right will be black hills of coal.

If you wish to see a natural, undeveloped hot springs, watch for the Lime Creek Mine turn-off at kilometre 17.8 (mile 11). You can see the Lime Creek plant in the distance. Drive for 1.3 kilometres (0.8 miles) and turn north on Sulphur Springs Road. It is a gravel logging road so watch for trucks. Follow the road to a Y and take the left fork. At kilometre 12 (mile 7.4) you will come to another split. The right split is the Upper Sulphur Springs Road, the left is the Lower Sulphur Springs Road. Stop and get out of your vehicle and breathe deeply. You will know you are near the springs.

Take the Lower Sulphur Springs Road (the sign is hidden in the trees) and go down the hill into the valley. You can see the river flowing through its many channels. At 0.8 kilometres (0.5 miles) you reach a road that runs off to the left. Turn onto it. You will go through an old burn area for about 0.5 kilometre (0.3 miles), then into the bush. The road is barely a vehicle width with big pot-holes. In about another 0.5 kilometre (0.3 miles) you come to a wide meadow.

At one time this was a campsite, and some decaying picnic tables remain. There are channels of water and an earth dam, with culverts to allow some flow, makes a small pool. An old wooden bridge crosses one part of the pool. White scum sits on the water and the rotten egg smell is very strong. The water is not very warm in the springs and bathing in them is not recommended unless you can have a shower afterwards.

For those who want to do some back country, high mountain driving take the Upper Sulphur Springs Road. If offers a great view over the valley. In a few kilometres (or miles) you come to a logging landing and trail in to Lost Lake.

If you have a power boat and want to do some fishing, instead of turning right to return to the highway when you get back to the Lime Creek road, continue ahead and drive to Grave Lake. This lake is the only one in the valley where motor boats are allowed. Land-locked kokanee are plentiful in the lake.

Fifteen kilometres (9 miles) from the Lime Creek Mine Road is Elkford. Elkford is called 'the Wilderness Capital of British Columbia.' One of North America's largest populations of bighorn sheep is found in the area. The Elk River runs through Elkford and has an abundance of Rocky Mountain whitefish, cutthroat and Dolly Varden. If you are in the area in late June and July, you will probably catch cutthroat. Fall is when the Dolly Varden bite best. You can spincast or fly-fish in the river.

Path to Josephine Falls

To reach Josephine Falls, drive to the four-way stop on the highway downtown and turn right. The road is paved and you cross a bridge and begin climbing and twisting your way up. At kilometre 5.4 (mile 3.3), watch for the small signs for Josephine Falls. It is a sharp right-hand turn off the pavement into the parking lot. You can hear water running as soon as you step out of your vehicle. Although the trail follows the river, you don't see it until you reach the falls.

Rustic benches at Josephine Falls

The 2.3 kilometre (1.4 mile) hiking trail is a lovely walk through the tall forest. Along the way you will cross bridges made of poles and there are pole benches to sit on to rest or to enjoy the scenery. Four interpretive signs tell about the vegetation, small animals, wildflowers and animal tracks. The trail is relatively easy with a few steep sections.

At the falls there is a viewpoint. The view here is not the best, so follow the beautiful canyon past the Lily Lake and Lost Lake signs and you will come to a better view where you can see the whole falls. If you wish to hike further, you can carry on to the other two lakes.

As you drive back towards Elkford, stop in at the Greenhills Viewpoint on the right. The road runs parallel to the highway, then makes a loop so that you can see the valley and Elkford below and the mountains across. The view is magnificent and well worth the few minutes it takes.

Besides downhill skiing in the winter, snowmobiling is a popular sport. Elkford's Snowmobile Association has developed a wide range of trails throughout the upper Elk Valley. Riders from the West Kootenays, Alberta and even the USA can travel trails into the valley on their machines. Access trails approved by the RCMP and the District of Elkford allow snowmobilers to start out from their homes or the hotel, gas up their machines, and then travel out of town.

Two roads lead north of Elkford. One is paved and heads northeast into the mountains. At one time this road was supposed to meet up with Highway 40 in Kananaskis Country in Alberta. So far, that

Canyon at Josephine Falls

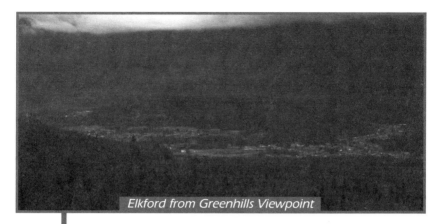
Elkford from Greenhills Viewpoint

has not happened. Although it is a dead end, the road does follow the Fording River, which offers great fishing for Dolly Varden, trout and Rocky Mountain whitefish.

The other road is gravel and heads north to Elk Lakes Provincial Park. With eight recreational areas along this road, there is plenty of camping. Elk Lakes is a wilderness park so bring everything you will need for your stay. The road has been upgraded and is two lanes most of the way. You travel on the west side of the Elk River until kilometre 48 (mile 30), when the road crosses it and joins the Kananaskis Power Line Road. From here it is another 25 kilometres (15.5 miles) to the park.

THE FRENCH MILITARY GROUP

Mount Nivelle, Mount Foch, the Petain Glacier and the Castelneau Glacier are just some of the names given to the mountains and glaciers in Elk Lakes Provincial Park. Nivelle, Foch, Petain and Castelneau were all French leaders in the First World War. These mountains, along with the other mountains and glaciers in the park named for First World War French commanders, are known as the French Military Group.

SPARWOOD

Back in Sparwood, that gigantic green truck with the huge black tires along the highway beside the information booth is the world's largest dump truck. It is called the Terex Titan truck and weighs 350 tonnes (385 tons), which got it into the Guinness Book of Records. It was used in coal mining for years but has now been retired.

Mural at Sparwood

You can see one of Sparwood's murals on the side of the information booth. To see the others, turn left when you leave the information booth parking lot and then turn right onto Red Cedar Drive. There are murals on the Overwaitea Store, on the Express Mart and on the church across from the Express Mart. This last one is of a wedding.

If you are here during July and August, take in a mine tour. You will see Canada's largest open-pit mine and some of the world's largest equipment shovelling and hauling the coal.

CANOEING THE ELK RIVER

The Elk River has four sections that are great for novice paddlers and whitewater rafters. All have Grade I and II rapids. (See p. 51 for an explanation of river grades.) Section 1 begins at the southeast side of the Elk River bridge in Hosmer. It is 9 kilometres (5.6 miles) long and can be ended at your choice of either the north bridge or the south bridge in Fernie.

Section 2 begins at either of the above bridges and is 4.5 kilometres (2.8 miles) from Fernie to the ski hill rapids. This section is also used by tire-tubers to beat the summer heat. You can take out at the Fernie Snow Valley Resort Road or continue 8.5 kilometres (5.3 miles) on Section 3 to the bridge at Morrissey. Section 4 begins at Morrissey Provincial Park and is 14 kilometres (8.7 miles) through a remote stretch of woods and hills. Make sure you take out at the bridge crossing the Elk River Reservoir at Elko. To go further will take you to the dangerous BC Hydro dam.

Fernie Museum in Roman Catholic Rectory

Fernie began as a coal town when the railway was put through the valley in 1890. It, too, has a disastrous past. In 1902, 128 men were killed in an explosion in the mine. Two years later, fire destroyed much of the town. In 1908, 23 men were trapped in the Coal Creek Mine explosion. The day after the explosion, a fire burning west of the town was fanned by winds and swept through the buildings, levelling almost everything. The townspeople only had time to save themselves. The fire continued up the valley and destroyed Sparwood. Fernie was rebuilt, this time of brick and stone, but the tragedy continued. In 1917, 34 men were killed in another Coal Creek Mine explosion.

Because of the use of brick and stone, many historic buildings survive today. A map is available at the information centre for a walking tour of the early buildings. The only chateau-style courthouse

Fernie City Hall, built in 1905

in the province was completed in 1911. It is on 4th Avenue between 4th and 5th Streets. The building that now houses the City Hall on 3rd Avenue between 5th and 6th Streets was built of brick and stone in 1905. It was the head office of the Crow's Nest Pass Coal Company and survived the 1908 fire along with 500 residents who sought refuge within its walls. The last surviving 'first class' railway station is on 1st Avenue between 6th and 7th Streets. It was declared a BC heritage site in 1985 and is now called the Arts Station. It has a theatre, photo lab, craft studio and gallery.

As you leave Fernie you travel beside the Elk River.

CROWSNEST PASS TO CRESTON **77**

ELKO TO CRANBROOK

ELKO AND KIKOMUN CREEK PROVINCIAL PARK

South of Fernie is Elko, on the northern end of Tobacco Plains. Thirty-one kilometres (19 miles) from Elko is the turn-off to Kikomun Creek Provincial Park and the Koocanusa Marina.

There is a parking area with a sign explaining where the sites of the park are. As you enter the park from the parking lot, immediately to your left is the road to Surveyor's Campground. To see some BC turtles, keep going straight ahead and you will see a sign 'Turtle Crossing.' Drive carefully through here because turtles might be on the road.

Hidden Lake, just past the sign, has a population of western painted turtles. These turtles are named for the colourful underside of their shells. You can pull

Western painted turtle at Kikomun Provincial Park

Lake Koocanusa

into the small parking lot, watching for turtles, and walk to the lake. You might see one or two turtles sitting on a log, or along the shore, or even swimming in the clear water near the edge. Go slowly or you will scare them from their perches on the logs.

For easy access to this lake while you are camping, take one of the campsites numbered 1 to 20. When you turn into the Surveyor's Campground you will come to a T. Turn right and follow it around the curve. Here are the numbers 1 to 20 and right behind them is the lake.

For a great view of Koocanusa Lake – named for the Kootenay River, Canada and the USA – continue on the road past Hidden Lake. At the end of the road is a picnic area and a hilltop view of the lake. Koocanusa Lake is the reservoir for the Libby Dam in Montana and is fed by the Elk and Kootenay rivers. Anglers will want to try for the kokanee, trout and Dolly Varden in the lake.

LOST GOLD: THE LEGEND OF THE LOST LEMON MINE

In 1870, Jack Lemon and his friend Blackjack left the Tobacco Plains in Montana to look for gold. After wandering through the mountains and foothills of Alberta for most of the summer and fall, they discovered a rich gold deposit. With winter approaching, they argued about staying and working their strike or staking it and returning in the spring. They fell asleep, the argument unresolved.

Lemon awoke during the night and, still angry, attacked Blackjack with an axe. Racked with guilt and bordering on insanity at his deed, he returned to Tobacco Plains and confessed to a priest. He gave directions to the claim to the priest who sent a man named John MacDougald to the murder site. MacDougald buried Blackjack, put a marker on the grave, and returned to Tobacco Plains.

According to the legend, the murder had been seen by two members of the Stoney band and they told the rest of the tribe. Knowing what a gold rush would mean to their territory, the band swore never to discuss the claim with anyone. They removed all signs of the grave and camp, and the gold has never been found again even though prospectors have searched north from the Crowsnest to Elk Lakes Provincial Park and east and west of this line.

GALLOWAY AND JAFFRAY

Fish at the Kootenay Trout Hatchery

West of Elko on Highway 3 are Galloway and Jaffray. Watch for the turn-off to the Bull River/Kootenay Fish Hatchery. This hatchery is one of six in the province, and kokanee, rainbow, lake trout, Dolly Varden, brook and Yellowstone cutthroat are raised here. The hatchery is open for tours from 8 am to 4 pm, but if you are late you can still watch fish swimming in a pool in front of the building.

CRANBROOK

In Cranbrook, the Canadian Museum of Rail Travel has the largest collection of railway passenger cars in North America – 12 restored cars in all. Seven of these cars make up the only complete set of the CPR's Trans-Canada Limited, a custom-made train designed and built in Canada in 1929. Here too is the *Strathcona*, the 1927 CP executive night car that has transported such dignitaries as Queen Elizabeth while she was still a princess, the Prince of Wales who as King Edward VIII abdicated his throne, and Sir Winston Churchill. To find the museum, continue on Highway 3 through town to the west end and it is on the right.

Canadian Museum of Rail Travel in Cranbrook

Cranbrook has a population of over 18,000 people and was named after the English hometown of an early settler named James Baker. The town owes its life to the CPR building its line through the community in 1898. The oldest building is the Colonel James Baker House which was built in 1889 and can be seen on the walking tour.

Cranbrook calls itself the sunniest town in B.C., with an average of 2244 hours of sunshine annually.

Fourteen kilometres (8.7 miles) southwest of Cranbrook on Highway 3 you cross the Moyie River for the first time and come to the Moyie Campground. The Moyie Lake Provincial Park turn-off is at kilometre 15.7 (mile 9.8) and just past that you cross the Moyie River again. Soon you begin twisting and turning you way alongside Moyie Lake.

MOYIE TO CRESTON

MOYIE AND YAHK

The once-rich mining industry in this area began when a Kutenai named Pierre found galena silver in the hills in 1893. Some of the old buildings or old building sites in Moyie are numbered for a walking tour. One building that will impress you is the old red fire hall on the left side of the road coming into town. It was built in 1907.

Moyie Fire Hall

Two kilometres (1.2 miles) west of Moyie you come to Moyie Lake again. The lake is made up of two sections, each about 6 kilometres (3.7 miles) long and joined by 2 kilometres (1.2 miles) of the Moyie River.

Along this lake is a combination of wet and dry belts. Cedar, Engelmann spruce and western hemlock prefer moister climates, while the ponderosa pine and Douglas-fir are found in drier areas. Actually, the southeastern part of British Columbia has the province's most abundant variety of flora and fauna.

Five kilometres (3.1 miles) from Moyie you cross the Moyie River and at kilometre 19 (mile 11.8) you come to the time-zone change so set your watch back one hour. Kilometre 26 (mile 16.2) brings you to the Moyie River again. As you pass through here, the Yahk Range of the Purcells is on your left and the Moyie Range is on your right.

Yahk stretches along the highway and while passing through you cross the Moyie River. The hotel is a heritage building, and during Prohibition, Yahk was a well-used meeting site for the whiskey runners.

Two kilometres (1.2 miles) from Yahk is the Moyie River again and just past the junction to the Kingsgate border crossing is the final bridge over the Moyie River.

ERICKSON

Erickson has a great abundance of fruit and produce stands, and you can see a number of orchards. Watch for the Wayside Garden and Arboretum on your left as you travel through town. There are

Wayside Garden and Arboretum In Erickson

2 hectares (5 acres) of trees, shrubs, lawn and pathways. Streams flow under arched bridges and there are water lily and fish ponds. floral displays include a rose garden, perennial borders, the rhododendron dell and lily beds. A gazebo stands on the lawn and benches are set out under the tall trees. There also is a teahouse and gift shop.

Anyone who lives in the area should buy a season pass because the flowers constantly change as old ones die and new ones blossom. The price to visit and look around is very reasonable and you can spend as long as you wish relaxing there.

CRESTON

Kutenai canoe, Creston Museum

On reaching Creston, turn left off Highway 3 at the set of lights on 17th Avenue, just past the Tourist Information Centre and head down to Erickson Street. Turn right and drive until you see the Columbia Brewery on your right. Kokanee Beer is brewed there, and tours are offered at 11:30 am, 1 pm and 2:30 pm on weekdays during the summer.

The Creston Museum is in the 'Stone House' on Devon Road near the west end of town. Turn off Highway 3 onto Devon Road and cross the railway tracks. The museum is on the left and parking is on the right.

A must to see is the Kutenai canoe. These distinctive canoes used to be made of pine bark, but when non-Natives came the Native people discovered that canvas obtained from the newcomers was easier to work with and easier to get. The canoe in the museum is made of green canvas and is one of only two canoes left of this type. The last Native who knew the art of building them, a woman named Charlotte Basil of the Creston Lower Kutenai Band, has passed away and no one else has taken it up.

The other Kutenai canoe is at the Royal British Columbia Museum in Victoria. It was built by the Kutenai Band of Creston for Expo '86.

The Candle Factory is in a grey building with green trim on the left side of the road as you head out of Creston. The factory makes candles from paraffin wax obtained from Ontario and beeswax from Alberta. The candles come in a wide variety of different shapes and types, including tapers, twisted, scented, praying hands and Christmas. The factory's business is 75% wholesale, but there is a gift shop. You can also tour the workshop and watch molds being put together to make more candles.

In case you are still wondering, 'Moyie' comes from the French word *mouille*, which means 'wet'; because of the dampness of the area, it was applied to the whole valley.

CRESTON, NELSON, TRAIL LOOP

Pilot Bay Lighthouse on Kootenay Lake

CRESTON, NELSON, TRAIL LOOP

This very scenic trip begins at Creston and heads north along the southern portion of Kootenay Lake. Because of the many summer and year-round residences, resorts and sights along the lake, signs along the highway warn of congested areas. The route crosses Kootenay Lake by ferry and goes west along the western arm of the lake. Then it zigzags from town to town before ending up back at Creston.

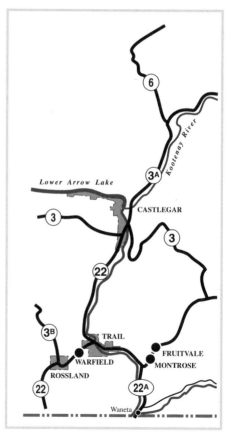

CRESTON TO KOOTENAY BAY

WYNNDEL, SIRDAR AND BOSWELL

At the west end of Creston, take Highway 3A north towards the ferry across Kootenay Lake. This road winds beside the lake and the speed limit is 80 kilometres (50 miles) per hour or less. Because of the residences in between, the towns all seem to blend together.

The road follows the Creston Valley. At kilometre 2.8 (mile 1.7) is a viewpoint overlooking the very beautiful valley. You can look down at the farms, the fields and the Kootenay River. Here, also, is a covered picnic site built out over the edge of the hill and supported

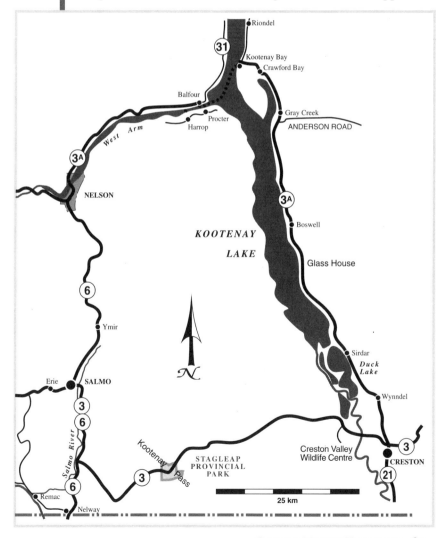

Covered picnic area overlooking Creston Valley

by posts. While enjoying the view over the valley, you can eat some of the fruit you bought earlier.

In spite of his failure at Canal Flats, British sportsman W.A. Baillie-Grohman decided to try to reclaim this land from the lake in 1893. He built canals to drain off the water and today 85 kilometres (53 miles) of dikes are used to keep the water away from 10,160 hectares (25,110 acres) of land.

As you travel Highway 3A, you get lovely glimpses of the Creston Valley to your left. You come to the Wynndel Irrigation District and then reach Wynndel itself.

Birdwatchers can stop along Duck Lake and look for the only colony of Forester's tern in British Columbia and the second largest nesting colony of the western grebe, an endangered bird. Six Mile Slough is west of Duck Lake; they both teem with marsh wrens, sora rails, blackbirds, great blue herons and ospreys. Duck Lake also has some of the best small mouth and large mouth bass fishing in western Canada.

The Sirdar Pub, across the road from Duck Lake at Sirdar, offers great home-cooked meals. Ye Olde Store next door has groceries.

If you wish to put a boat on Kootenay Lake, at kilometre 24.2 (mile 15) is a rest area with a boat launch. Do not pull into the first road – that is the exit. Go past that and into the second.

The Glass House, at kilometre 38.4 (mile 23.9), was built by David H. Brown, a retired funeral director. After discovering that it was possible to build a house out of glass bricks, he began collecting embalming fluid bottles from funeral homes in western Canada. In 1952, when he had 500,000 bottles weighing 225 tonnes (250 tons), he began construction of

Glass House

Kootenay Lake

his 111 square metre (1200 square foot) home on the solid rock of the Kootenay lakeshore.

In the yard, you will see a stream gurgling over a water wheel, a bridge also made of bottles, a pathway leading to a replica of a lighthouse, and a 10.7 metre (35 foot) high observation tower that you can climb on a spiral stairway. Inside on the main floor of the house are three circular rooms (the living room, kitchen and master bedroom).

Brown died in 1970, but his family opens the house to the public between May 1 and Thanksgiving weekend. And speaking of Thanksgiving, watch for wild turkeys along the side of the road through here.

Boswell, further north along the lake, is where the Beadman makes his home. Anyone who likes to make crafts using beads or who likes bead jewellery should stop in and see his huge bead collection. Congestion occurs in many areas along this part of the route, so watch for the signs.

CROSS COUNTY TO KIMBERLEY

Anderson Road, just south of Gray Creek, is a high-mountain backroad to Kimberley. This winding and steep 85 kilometre (52.8 mile) road is gravel for 70.8 kilometres (44 miles). The first 15 kilometres (9.3 miles) is a 14% climb to the summit of the Purcells at 2028 metres (6653 feet). Don't be surprised to see snow in August.

It shortens the trip from Kootenay Lake to Calgary by 80 kilometres (50 miles) but, because of the slower speeds, it is not faster. A summer road only, it was completed in 1991. Opening dates depend on the weather.

GRAY CREEK, CRAWFORD BAY AND KOOTENAY BAY

Gray Creek is where the gold boulder, a large nugget of gold that sparked another BC gold rush, was found. The Gray Creek Store has been open since 1913 and is the oldest and largest general store on Kootenay Lake. For a bit of nostalgia, step inside, walk on the old wooden floorboards and inhale the mixture of smells. There are shelves of modern and not so modern items, and towards the back is a room with hardware and wood stoves. If you don't know what an object is, and it is not labelled, ask the owner. Out in the yard is an old hand-operated gas pump beside the driveway.

Crawford Bay has a variety of craftspeople. One of the more unusual crafts is the making of straw brooms. At the north end of the hamlet is the North Woven Broom Co. in a brown log barn on the right side of the road. The smell inside the barn is sweet from the sorghum straw brought in from Mexico.

Hand-operated gas pump at Gray Creek Store

The company makes brooms of various sizes: from whisks and small, round brooms designed by the local golf club for sweeping golf shoes, to the long-handled, regular straw brooms that everyone knows and recognizes. One of the best sellers is an old style with untrimmed straw and the curved, wooden Manzanita branch handle. This type dates back before 1840.

North Woven Broom Co. is the only traditional broom factory in the West. The brooms are made according to 19th-century methods. A 100-year-old stitcher is used to sew the larger brooms flat but the whisk and crooked handle broom are all handstitched with the aid of an antique vise. You can watch as the brooms are being made and then buy the product. The company is open 11 months of the year, closing only in December to stock up on the broom supply.

Gray Creek Store

Just past the broom company, on the left side of the road, is a working smithy called the Kootenay Forge and Blacksmith Shop. You can stand in the doorway and watch as the blacksmith heats the metal to about 1100°C (2000°F) in the

North Woven Broom Co. in Crawford Bay

forge and then places it on an anvil and shapes it with a hammer. There is a gift shop where you can buy spice racks, candleholders, fireplace accessories, door knockers and much more.

About 2 kilometres (1.2 miles) from the blacksmith shop is the turn-off to Riondel. The

THE BLUEBELL MINE

In 1882 Robert Evan Sproule staked the Bluebell on an outcrop that had been used by Native peoples and fur traders for years as a source of lead for bullets. Three other men with him also staked claims in the area. However, they had not brought enough food for their stay and in early fall the three half-starved men left. This was serious because according to the BC mining laws, miners could not leave their claim from June to the end of October without permission from the Gold Commissioner. Sproule tried to stay to the end of the month but with only flour left to eat, had to leave on October 24. Before he left he tacked a note on the Bluebell stake explaining his predicament and stating that he would return in the spring.

As soon as he left, Thomas Hammill, who had been watching the miners, declared the claims abandoned. He restaked them in his men's names and began to work them. Sproule and the other men returned in the spring to find their claims gone. They took the claim jumpers to court and the judge found in their favour.

Hammill appealed to a higher court and won the other men's claims back but Sproule maintained his. However, in order to pay his lawyer, Sproule deeded him one-third of the claim. In a twist of fate, the lawyer, also in need of money, sold his share to Thomas Hammill. Sproule, outraged, stated that he would fix Hammill if he ever set foot on the claim.

On June 1, 1885 Thomas Hammill was shot in the back while working the Bluebell claim. Sproule was tried for the murder in Victoria, found guilty and sentenced to hang. A furor was raised by jurors and witnesses and a public meeting was held in Victoria with a full review of the case demanded.

The day of execution was delayed three times owing to the legal battles but finally on October 29, 1886, Sproule was led to the gallows and hanged.

road is paved and it climbs above the lake. When you enter Riondel, turn left towards the campground. At Eastman Avenue, turn right. About half a block down the road is an open area with a sign describing the Bluebell Mine.

While in Riondel, take the Waterfront Trail, which follows the Kootenay Lake shoreline for 1.5 kilometres (0.9 miles) to the original mine site on Blue Bell Bay. The trail begins at the south end of the North Bay Beach Campground. You will pass stone foundations, all that is left of the tent community that housed the Bluebell miners in the 1880s.

If you don't take the Riondel trip, stay on Highway 3A and just past the Riondel turn-off you descend down to Kootenay Bay and the ferry. Drive slowly.

If you have the time, turn left onto Pilot Bay Road and follow it for 4.6 kilometres (2.9 miles) to the sign for the Pilot Bay Light-house Trail. It is a blue sign with white printing nailed to a white post. The walk is through tall trees and is steep in places. In about 10 minutes you reach the white lighthouse with red trim, perched on the edge of the cliff above the lake.

If the door is open, go in and look around. There is a set of steep red stairs that you can climb to the second storey, and an even steeper set of steps up to the top. At the top you have a magnificent view out over the lake.

Ferry over Kootenay Lake

To take pictures without having to look through the streaked and dirty glass, close the trap door at the top of the stairs and push open the door leading to the ledge around the top. The ledge has a slight slope to it but there is a railing around it. To get back down you will have to back down the steps to the second level, and it is up to you if you go down front or back to the ground floor. Entering the lighthouse and climbing out on the ledge is at your own risk, so be careful.

The ferry ride across Kootenay Lake, which takes 40 minutes, is the longest free ferry ride in North America. While on board, look ahead at the Selkirks or behind for a great view of the Purcell Mountains. To the northwest is Kokanee Glacier.

BALFOUR TO YMIR

BALFOUR

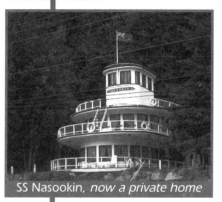
SS Nasookin, *now a private home*

Balfour is a small community with plenty of campsites and restaurants. At Langs, just to the right as you get off the ferry, you can buy some grain to feed the flock of Canada geese on the beach. Straight ahead from the ferry is a T intersection. Turn left to Nelson. From Balfour you will follow the north shore of the west arm of Kootenay Lake. The *Globe and Mail* calls this road one of the most scenic routes in Canada.

KOOTENAY LAKE

Kootenay Lake is 145 kilometres (90 miles) long and is one of British Columbia's most important freshwater fisheries. The world's largest kokanee, an inland salmon that spawns in the Kokanee Creek, lives in this lake. They swim up the creek to spawn in late August and early September. Gerrard rainbow trout from this lake can weigh up to 10 kilograms (22 pounds). The Gerrard is the largest species of rainbow trout in the world. They can grow to 13 kilograms (29 pounds) or more. Any one wishing to try for these mighty fish must purchase a Kootenay Lake rainbow trout licence.

This lake is great for people who like winter fishing without the ice. It does not freeze during the winter and trophy rainbow up to 15 kilograms (33 pounds) have been caught.

At kilometre 6.3 (mile 3.9) from Balfour is the Harrop/Proctor ferry. If you are a scuba diver you might want to take the ferry across to Harrop. On Fairbank Road is the Down Under Diving Shop, where you can rent gear and get information about diving sites on Kootenay Lake.

This section of Highway 3A, like most British Columbia roads, has many curves in it. When you come around one of these curves you see a paddlewheeler sitting high and dry across the road from the lake. It is white with red trim and is an authentic paddlewheeler. The SS *Nasookin* worked Kootenay Lake for many years and then was used as an automobile ferry by the government from 1933 to 1947. It is now a private residence.

NELSON

Cable car #23 in Nelson

As soon as you cross the bridge over the west arm of Kootenay Lake into Nelson, take the first right and go down to the Lakeside Park. At the yield sign, turn right and follow the road to the tram.

When the Nelson Electric Tramway Company began operation in 1899, it was the smallest electric streetcar system in the British Empire. It ran through the downtown district, climbed up to the residential section, and then out to the shipyards near the park. You can ride on car #23, which was built in 1906 and came to Nelson from Cleveland, Ohio in 1924. It was restored in the 1980s and will take you by the Chahko-Mika mall, to the wharf at the end of Hill Street, and then back to the park the same way.

If the tram is out on a trip, spend some time in the park. Benches are along the lakeshore and under the tall, shady trees, and there is a playground for the children.

Nelson is the centre of a large area of placer (pronounced like 'plaster' but without the 't') and commercial mining. Anyone wanting to stake a placer claim must get a Free Miner certificate from the Gold Commissioner's office in Nelson. If you are interested in mining, visit the Chamber of Mines of Eastern BC It has maps and reports that go back as far as 1895, a mining library and a geological museum. Originally founded in 1926 to prevent claim jumping, it now is a research library for prospectors. It is open 1 pm to 5 pm on weekdays.

When silver was discovered on Toad Mountain in 1887, Nelson was quickly established nearby to accommodate the men of the Silver King Mine. Besides silver, gold and coal were also discovered in the area. The town was incorporated in 1897 and was the largest city between Vancouver and Winnipeg by 1904.

During the end of the last century, Nelson expanded uphill owing to the lack of flat land along the river. Over the years the town has preserved its buildings, and now it has the second largest number of historical buildings in Canada. Visit the Nelson courthouse, which was built of Kootenay marble with bits of gold embedded in it. There is a historic driving tour of the houses and businesses up the hill and a walking tour of the buildings on the flatter section of the city.

YMIR

Ymir Hotel

South of Nelson on Highway 6 is the town of Ymir (pronounced 'why mer'). At the second of two entrances into Ymir is a mural on a huge sign to welcome you as you turn in. The old Ymir Hotel, built in 1896, is still standing. It now has a metal roof and the first floor front and sides have been changed, but the second and third storeys are still the same.

Ymir was known as Quartz Creek in 1892 when it began as the water-tank stop for the Nelson & Fort Sheppard Railway. In 1897 it was surveyed and renamed Ymir. It had a wild beginning, with owners of hotels being evicted by anyone who wanted to take over, rooms being broken into and shots being fired, men robbing the dead, fires and suicides.

In 1901, gold bricks worth $40,000 (at the time) were being turned out at the Ymir mine, and for a brief time it was the largest mine in the British Empire. During the First World War many of the mines in the area closed down. They reopened in the 1930s and 1940s when the price of gold was high but the town never regained its prosperity, remaining much as it is today.

'WHY AM I HERE?'
Early settlers, after travelling thousands of miles, arrived in the area and decided to build a town on this site. Some time later, one of them, after having a bad day, looked around and asked in exasperation 'Why am I here?' That became everyone's expression on a hard day and soon it was reduced to Ymir, thus giving the town its name.

SALMO TO TRAIL

SALMO AND ERIE

Rock mural, Salmo Museum
(photo by F. Olive Donaldson)

Salmo, south of Ymir, is the home of Penny Power. One day the townspeople decided to start collecting pennies. Over the months of the project they filled barrels and barrels with them. The reason? On July 1, 1995, they sent all the pennies to the government in Ottawa to help reduce the national debt. When they began the project they issued a challenge to other communities to do the same but none of them collected as many as did the people of Salmo.

The murals on the walls in Salmo are unusual. They are made of coloured rock and were done by the students of the local Kootenay

World's oldest telephone booth
(photo by F. Olive Donaldson)

Stone Training Institute. The students drew the picture on the wall then cemented the different colours of rock in place.

The old Salmo Hotel has a mural that shows miners of years ago inside a mine shaft. On the back of the museum is a large picture of a prospector kneeling beside a river checking his pan for gold. One block north is a mural of two lumberjacks cutting down a tree. In this one the tree trunk is rounded out, giving it a three-dimensional look. This town has done a beautiful and unique job with its murals.

Just as you turn west onto Highway 3 you will come to Trapper John's Restaurant and the Sal-Crest Motel. In the motel yard is a cedar tree trunk with a telephone in it. At 400 years of age, this tree trunk is the world's oldest telephone booth. Go into the motel office and see the map of Canada, dated 1901.

THE FIRST MURDER

Salmo was originally known as Salmon City and was the scene of the first murder in the area. In October 1893, after a night of poker, the players decided to call it quits. They stood to go but one man, Charlie Ross, claimed he had lost a cheque and wanted to search the other players. They agreed.

While he was searching a man named Steven Hamlin, who had come to town a few days earlier in possession of a considerable amount of money, another man named William O'Brien started to leave. Hamlin stopped him and after a few words, punched him. O'Brien struck back, knocking Hamlin down. O'Brien then kicked Hamlin twice in the head before being stopped. Hamlin was revived but was unable to stand.

A day later, when it was apparent that Hamlin would not survive, O'Brien and the other men of the game carried him to their cabin to look after him. However, they took off to the United States, leaving Hamlin to die alone. None of Hamlin's money was found.

PROSPECTING

During the 1930s, many prospectors lived in cabins near Salmo River; the remains of these cabins can still be found. Gold was found by scraping the walls of the crevasses along the river.

At kilometre 3.2 (mile 2) you come to Erie. On the right is the Selkirk Motel and Campground. The campground stays open in the fall until the water lines freeze up.

CASTLEGAR

After turning right towards Castlegar at the junction with Highway 3B, you begin a long, steep climb that lasts to the Bombi Summit (elevation 1214 metres [3983 feet]). On the descent you have a great view of Castlegar and the valley.

To see the Doukhobor Museum, you take the Airport/Nelson Road and then watch for the signs to the museum. Exhibits and buildings show Doukhobor history and lifestyle in Russia and Canada. It is a model community village complete with a blacksmith shop, handmade tools, a bread oven and a wood-heated bath house. You can sample some Doukhobor cooking, such as borscht and perogies, at the Spinning Wheel Eatery, where all the dishes are vegetarian.

Doukhobor Museum, Castlegar

DOUKHOBORS

The name Doukhobor comes from Doukhobortsi, *which was given to these people in 1785 and means 'spirit wrestlers.' Although they accepted the name (which was meant disparagingly), they changed the meaning to 'We are spirit wrestlers because we wrestle with and for the Spirit of God.'*

The Doukhobors had strong religious beliefs, were vegetarians and lived in a structured commune. They were also pacifists and refused to serve in the military in czarist Russia. Hence, they were persecuted in their home country and finally, with the help of writer Leo Tolstoy and the Quakers, they left Russia for Canada.

Led by their spiritual leader, Peter Verigin, they first settled in Alberta and Saskatchewan, but problems with the governments in these provinces forced them to move to central British Columbia.

Suspension bridge to Zuckerberg Island

Next to the Doukhobor Museum is the West Kootenay National Exhibition Centre, which is one of 23 such centres in Canada. Throughout the year, displays are put on by local as well as international cultures. The centre is the only public gallery in the Kootenays that is able to attract large travelling exhibitions of art, history and science. Besides the gallery there is a gift shop with a wide range of crafts.

To reach Zuckerberg Island Heritage Park, turn right on the road to the airport and Nelson and then right again on Highway 3 and drive to Columbia Avenue. Turn right, go to 9th Street and turn right yet again. Follow it to the river and the parking lot.

You can get to the island by way of the suspension bridge built by the 44th Firled Engineer Squadron in 1944, or you can walk across the causeway. There is a circle tour of the outer edge of

Chapel House

the island on which you will see the water wheel site, the bird habitat and the western yew tree, which was sought after for bows, gun stocks and musical instruments. Hiking trails through the trees on the island take you to the sculptured stump lady, the Chapel House and the cemetery.

Alexander Feodorovitch Zuckerberg was a high school math teacher in Russia who came to Canada in 1921 with his wife and two children. In 1931 he moved to Castlegar to teach the Doukhobor children. He built a log house on the island to live in while he constructed the Chapel House styled after his home in Russia.

TRAIL AND WARFIELD

Comico Mine stack in Trail

Trail is south of Castlegar via Highway 22. On the left as you enter Trail is the Cominco Mine. You can see its smoke stacks from a long way. Trail was originally named Trail Creek Landing and began as a Columbia River port when gold-copper ore was discovered near Rossland around 1890. A small smelter was built in the late 1890s and in 1906 Cominco began operations.

This smelter is now the largest integrated lead-zinc smelter in the world. Besides the minerals it gets from BC mines, it also processes materials from other parts of the world. Some of the metals it produces are indium, germanium dioxide, zinc, cadmium, silver and gold; it also produces agricultural fertilizers. Visit the plant. Tours of about two hours are offered weekdays beginning at 10 am but children under 12 and cameras are not allowed.

Trail was the host city for the 1995 Babe Ruth World Series for 16–18 year-olds, the first time this series was held outside the United States. Babe Ruth baseball has over 850,000 players in 10,000 leagues and is North America's largest youth recreational program. In Canada, the town of Trail holds the honour of having participated in Babe Ruth baseball for the most number of years. Unfortunately, Trail did not win the tournament. That honour went to Vancouver, Washington.

As you come into Trail, turn right onto Rossland Avenue. Rossland Avenue, also known as 'The Gulch,' has one of British Columbia's largest collections of early 20th-century false-front buildings. Visit Star Grocery to see a wide selection of Italian foods.

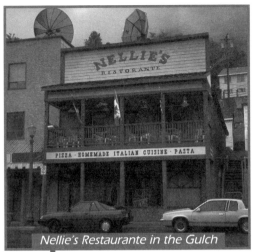
Nellie's Restaurante in the Gulch

Lauriente's Clothing Store at 730 Rossland Avenue is believed to be the first brick building in Trail and is one of the oldest businesses in the southern Interior.

The Gulch also was the heart of the Italian community. The first Italian to work at Cominco was Isaac Georgetti, who came to the area in 1895. Others followed soon after, taking jobs at the smelter, on the railway, or starting their own businesses. Many settled in West Trail. Rossland Avenue heads west to Rossland, and as you leave Trail the sign says *Arrivederci*.

Between Trail and Rossland is the town of Warfield. You can see the town spread out below and above you. Warfield has been given the name 'Mickey Mouse Town' because of the colourful, Disney-like homes that were built by Cominco in the 1930s.

ROSSLAND TO CRESTON

ROSSLAND

At kilometre 5.8 (mile 3.6) on the left is the turn-off for the Rossland Golf Course. Try a round here, not because it is set in a beautiful valley of trees or even because you might see an occasional deer wander across the fairway, but because of the par three, 119 metre (130 yard) hole with the rope tow. If you don't think you can make the hike up from the tee to the green, press the button, grab hold of the rope, and it will pull you up.

When you reach the flashing light in Rossland, turn left and you are on Columbia Avenue. The street is very clean and old fashioned with antique street lamps and little brown signs telling you where you can park. Dog owners should note that no dogs are allowed on Rossland's main street.

The old Bank of Montreal building is made of brown brick, and you can drive up and down any street in the main section of Rossland and see heritage homes and buildings.

Heritage building in Rossland

Rossland is in the crater of an extinct volcano. It is 1023 metres (3410 feet) above sea level in the Monashee Mountains and 609 metres (2000 feet) above the City of Trail and the Columbia River.

The town was quickly established after two prospectors staked five claims on a mountain near the Dewdney Trail in 1890. These claims launched the discovery of the rich gold-copper ore in Red Mountain, just northwest of town, and led to the opening of the area. In 1896 the British Columbia Smelting and Refining Company was built on a bench of land above the town site of Trail Creek; the first gold brick was formed the next year.

LEROI MINE

In 1890 two men staked four claims on the eastern slopes of Red Mountain, northwest of present-day Rossland. Although each man was only allowed two claims, one staked an extra claim and called it the LeWise. When they went to Nelson to record their claims, the LeWise was given to the mine recorder, Eugene S. Topping, in lieu of the $12.50 recording fee for all five claims.

Topping recorded the claim under the name LeRoi and when ore from the claim was assayed it was the highest in the area. Topping went to Spokane and sold his claim to a syndicate for $35,000. In its lifetime from 1890 to 1929 the LeRoi produced $30 million worth of gold.

The gold produced from the Rossland area was more than that of all the placer rivers and creeks of BC combined.

By the beginning of the 1900s Rossland had a population of 7000 and was incorporated, with three breweries, five banks, seven newspapers, 17 law firms and 42 saloons which remained opened 24 hours a day. If a miner or visitor couldn't afford the $10 cost of a hotel room, he could rent a chair at the International Hotel for $1 and stay the night.

The Rossland Historical Museum has exhibits of the geological history of the area, a bottle room and a Chinese garden. From the museum you can take an underground tour of the LeRoi Gold Mine, the only genuine hardrock mine open to the public in Canada. Make sure you take a jacket because it is cold down there, and wear closed-in shoes or hiking boots. You will follow your guide into the Black Bear tunnel and walk down the main haulageway for 240 metres (800 feet) to the meeting of the LeRoi mine shaft 90 metres (300 feet) below ground. Your guide will take you through exploration tunnels and past displays of mining tools, and will point out veins and dikes.

The museum is also the home of the Western Canada Ski Hall of Fame in the Nancy Greene wing. Nancy Greene was the 1968 Downhill Skiing Gold Medallist and won the World Cup twice. To reach the museum, drive down Columbia Avenue to where it meets Highway 3B. The museum is on the right. Turn right onto Highway 3B and you will end up at Nancy Greene Provincial Park.

On your way back to Trail, you have another excellent view of Warfield and its old, quaint houses set along the hillside. On rainy days, this road has a tendency to get foggy in places. To get back into Trail you descend on a 10% grade. You drive through Trail and as you leave you cross the Columbia River on a four-lane bridge.

WANETA, MONTROSE AND FRUITVALE

Southeast of Trail, close to the USA border, is Waneta. The Waneta Plaza Shopping Mall, the largest mall in the Kootenays, is beside the highway. (To reach Canada Customs Waneta port of entry, turn right on Highway 22A.)

Further along, past Highway 22A, a roadside turnout gives you a view of the Beaver Valley. Montrose bills itself as the gateway to the Beaver Valley. You drive through Montrose, Beaver Falls and into Fruitvale as if they were one town.

Fruitvale began as a railway stop and was named Beaver Siding. In 1906 the Fruitvale Limited, a land corporation, bought land on both sides of the railway and renamed the stop Fruitvale.

At kilometre 17 (mile 10.6) from Highway 22A, start watching for a historic site sign. From it you go around a curve and come to a small log building on the right side of the road. This is the Park Siding School, built in 1912. It was moved to this site and put on a cement foundation in 1990. The door is unlocked so

Park Siding School, built in 1912

enter and look around. There is a cage at the entrance through which you can see how an old, one-room school looked. It has the rows of student desks, the teacher's desk, an old piano, a wood stove, and a wash stand and basin. Before you leave, sign the guest book.

REMAC

After passing the turn-off (Highway 3) to Castlegar, you once again reach the junction of Highways 3 and 6 at Salmo. Head south on Highway 3/6. You can see the Salmo River to your right. At about kilometre 9 (mile 5.6) you will pass a large berm with a house on top and at kilometre 10.4 (mile 6.5) to the right, you will see the remains of an old bridge that used to cross the Salmo River. The Salmo is a very popular and productive gold river and to reach the claims on the other side and downstream, prospectors have to do some high-mountain backroad driving.

At kilometre 13.8 (mile 8.6) from Salmo, keep right on Highway 6 where it leaves Highway 3 and drive south to the USA border at Nelway, but do not go through. As you reach the Customs building, there is a house on the right. Turn right onto the road beside the house. You will drive by a farm and then start climbing beside the beautiful, emerald-green Pend Oreille River. The cement ruins you see are what is left of the gold mining town of Remac. It closed in the 1950s and all the buildings were moved out.

You will cross a bailey bridge over the Salmo River as it pours into the Pend Oreille, and about 50 metres (164 feet) from the bridge there is a switchback road to the right. It immediately starts climbing above the road you were just on. This road takes you high alongside the Salmo River and to the Shenango Canyon.

THE DEPRESSION GOLD CLAIMS

During the Depression, most jobs went to a man with a family to support. The Canadian government encouraged young, single men to go placer mining, and offered a placer mining course by correspondence. After taking the course, Oliver Donaldson left the farm in the Qu'Appelle Valley of Saskatchewan and headed to BC to join his two brothers, Albert and Gilbert. Like so many young men, they had left home to eke out a living in the mountains of BC.

They staked claims along the Salmon River (now the Salmo) and built a log cabin on a bluff overlooking the river. Gold was worth $35 an ounce, and they managed to find enough flour gold each month to buy groceries. They shot deer, fished and picked berries to supplement their supplies. In the winters they either found work in the area or returned home to help on the farm.

There were other prospectors on the river, some of whom had been on the trail of '98 up to Dawson City. According to the brothers, when they walked past the old timers' cabins and yelled 'Hello' at them, on a good day the old guys would ignore them. On a bad day they would swear heartily back at them.

The Donaldson cabin burned but the bottom row of logs can still be seen on the cliff above the river.

KOOTENAY PASS

Kootenay Pass in June

Retrace your route to the junction of Highways 6 and 3. Head east to begin the long climb up to Kootenay Pass. This pass is the last hill before you reach Creston. Be sure to check your brakes before heading out, and if you are pulling a trailer, make sure it has brakes on it. On a rainy day, you will either be in fog or in the low clouds. If it is June or September, don't be surprised to find snow on the ground or still falling. In 23 kilometres (14.3 miles) you reach the Kootenay Pass summit at 1774 metres (5820 feet).

Creston Valley Wildlife Management Area

At the summit is a large turn-out beside a small lake, a hiker's cabin and Stagleap Provincial Park. Stagleap was named after the woodland caribou that migrate through this area, northeastern Washington, northern Idaho and sometimes northwestern Montana. It is the only herd of woodland caribou in the lower 48 states and is on the endangered species list. The animals can weigh 135–225 kilograms (300-500 pounds) and, with an 18 centimetre (7 inch) hoof, they are able to distribute their weight better and walk on snow easier.

From the summit, it is downhill all the way to Creston, and you will be using your brakes most of the way down. At kilometre 36 (mile 22.4) from the top you reach the turn to the Creston Valley Wildlife Centre. Shortly after the turn there is a 'Y' in the road. Take the left fork and you will come to the centre in just a kilometre (0.6 mile).

The Creston Valley Wildlife Management Area consists of 7000 hectares (17,000 acres) of wetlands, woods and mountains. You can canoe through the marshes, hike on one of the dikes or trails, watch for over 250 species of birds, or camp at the Summit Creek campground.

Inside the centre are murals, displays and material about the birds, reptiles, amphibians and mammals that live in the area. The centre, with its gift and coffee shops, is open from 8 am to 8 pm daily but the trails are open 24 hours.

Dykes built by W.A. Baillie-Grohman

On your way into Creston you cross a bridge over the Old Kootenay Channel. To the right you will see part of the 85 kilometres (53 miles) of dikes. Then you cross the Kootenay River itself and reach the junction where you started.

CHAPTER 6

AINSWORTH HOT SPRINGS, NAKUSP & THE SLOCAN VALLEY

Japanese Gardens on Nakusp Promenade

AINSWORTH HOT SPRINGS, NAKUSP & THE SLOCAN VALLEY

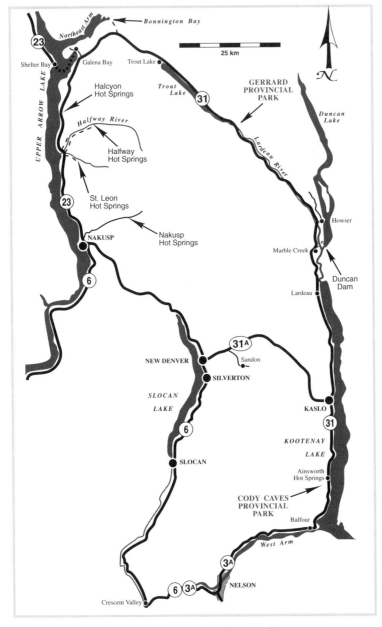

This route curves north from Ainsworth Hot Springs along the west side of Kootenay Lake, and then south along Upper Arrow and Slocan lakes through to Castlegar. Scenery is interspersed with mining history, Japanese culture, railway problems and hot springs.

AINSWORTH TO TROUT LAKE

AINSWORTH

Take Highway 31 north of Balfour, on the west arm of Kootenay Lake. Ainsworth Hot Springs are in an old mine shaft abandoned because the miners found more hot water than ore. According to legend, the Native people who discovered the springs around 1800 found animals standing or lying in the soothing waters, healing their wounds.

As you leave the changing rooms, you enter the horseshoe-shaped cave with its 45°C (113°F) temperature. Just outside is the Jacuzzi corner and then the main 32°C (90°F) pool out in the sunshine. After your soak, take a refreshing plunge in the cold pool. What you will notice is that there is not the sulphur smell usually associated with hot springs waters.

Ainsworth has two historic buildings. The J.B. Fletcher store on the corner of the highway and Sutton Street is open on weekends in May and June and daily in July and August. The building has been restored to its 1896 splendour. Besides artifacts from the mining era, it has the Kutenai Showcase with crafts from 40 local Native artists.

Just up the hill from the store is the Silver Ledge Hotel, which celebrated its 100th anniversary in 1996. (A 'ledge' is a vein of ore-bearing rock.) The building is now a museum.

Ainsworth Hot Springs

Two kilometres (1.2 miles) north of Ainsworth is the turn-off to Cody Caves. It is a sharp left-hand turn, and you immediately begin to climb. A sign at the beginning of the road states that it is not recommended for trailers or low-clearance vehicles. The road is steep, sometimes dirt and sometimes gravel, winding and narrow with sheer drop-offs, but you are driving through a park-like setting of tall trees and at times have splendid views of Kootenay Lake. You climb high enough that you are

J.B. Fletcher Store in Ainsworth

level with the mountain tops across the valley.

At kilometre 9 (mile 5.6), the hillside is covered by small rocky debris and timbers. The rocky debris is mine tailings – what's left after the ore is removed. There is a small creek, and if you climb into the bush on the left side of the creek as you face it, you will find some ruins of log buildings that were used during the mining era. At kilometre 11.3 (mile 7), you reach the Cody Caves parking lot. Here the mosquitoes are very bad; they are worse up at the caves.

Cody Caves were discovered by a prospector named Henry Cody in the late 1880s while he was searching for silver and gold. They became very popular after an 1899 article in *Argosy* magazine told about the gold-lined walls of a cave in the Ainsworth area. Needless to say, gold was not found.

Guided tours of the caves are available, and the tour guide provides all the supplies needed. To take a tour, phone Hiadventure Corp at (604) 353-7425. For information about the condition of the caves and road, phone BC Parks at (604) 825-3500. The caves are generally closed until mid-June depending on the weather.

Silver Ledge Hotel, Ainsworth

If you are travelling alone, you are advised not to enter the caves or even take the scenic 800 metre (875 yard) hike up to them. It might be awhile before you are discovered if you happen to fall. People exploring without a guide should be physically fit, wear good boots and warm cloth-

Mine remnants on road to Cody Caves

ing, have two or three flashlights per person, wear a hard hat (preferably with a chin strap), and have a strong rope.

Remember that the stalactites, soda straws, stalagmites and other formations you see in the caves are almost 600 million years old. They have grown at the imperceptible rate of one cubic centimetre per 100 years. They are fragile and if handled by a human hand will not grow further because of the oil deposited from that hand. Look, don't touch.

FISHING KOOTENAY LAKE

Kootenay Lake is world renowned for its trophy trout. The record Gerrard trout is 16.2 kilograms (35 pounds 12 ounces). Dolly Varden up to 6.8 kilograms (15 pounds) have also been caught there. The west arm at Balfour is famous for huge sturgeon.

Two of the best fishing areas are on the east side across from Kaslo Bay and around Coffee Creek, between Balfour and Ainsworth. The Bucktail fly has proven to be successful for catching rainbow, and different plugs appeal to the Dollies. At the Ainsworth Hot Springs Resort, look at the 11.1 kilogram (24 pounds 8 ounces) rainbow trout mounted on the lobby wall.

KASLO

Kaslo is a historic mining town north of Ainsworth. In 1892 a silver ore boulder worth $20,000 at the time was discovered south of Kaslo. An immediate boom gave the town over 20 hotels, 14 barber shops, two newspapers, a sawmill and a brewing company. The well-known and well-visited 'Theatre Comique' had 80 dancehall girls to keep the miners entertained. Two years after the boulder was discovered, a fire destroyed much of the town. It rebuilt and managed to survive the flooding of the Kaslo River and the fluctuating silver ore prices over the years. The town diversified, trying orchards and dairies to keep alive. Kaslo was the 21st town to incorporate in British Columbia and the first in the Kootenays. It celebrated its centennial in 1993.

SS Moyie *in Kaslo*

Look for the old paddle-wheeler, the *SS Moyie,* on Front Street beside the tourist information. Her steel hull was built in Toronto and shipped by rail to the West Coast. It was then sent to Nelson, where it was assembled with the rest of the paddlewheeler. The *SS Moyie* was launched from the dock in Nelson on October 22, 1898 as part of the CPR's Crow's Nest Pass Railway. She hauled freight and passengers until 1906 when the larger and faster *Kuskanook* replaced her.

After years of hauling tourists and supplies on Kootenay Lake, she was taken to Kaslo in 1957 and turned into a museum. Stroll her decks, check out the engine room with its rare equipment, and see the ladies' saloon. She is the oldest surviving vessel of her type in the world. And she holds the record for the longest service of any sternwheeler in Canada. If you are in Kaslo at noon, you will hear an original brass whistle blow that will put you back in the days of the sternwheeler.

The three-storey Langham Hotel was built in 1893 when there was a great shortage of beds for the miners. By the time it was completed in the summer, the demand for silver had decreased. It became a boarding house and rented out office space. The building now houses two galleries, a 90-seat theatre and two museums.

LARDEAU, MEADOW CREEK, HOWSER AND GERRARD

Twenty-eight kilometres (17.4 miles) north of Kaslo on Highway 31 is a T intersection. Turn right into Lardeau on Kootenay Lake. It is a nice little town with a boat launch. Three kilometres (1.9 miles) from Lardeau is the north end of Kootenay Lake.

Langham Hotel in Kaslo

WINTER BLIZZARD

The winter of 1934-35 is remembered for its heavy snowfall and blizzard. According to reports, 63.5 centimetres (25 inches) of snow fell in 24 hours. Roads were closed because of the blizzard, and avalanches blocked the railway. Since there was no snow removal, train service between Lardeau and Gerrard to the north had been suspended by the CPR, which had decided not to reopen the line again until late April.

The CPR's decision angered the inhabitants of the Lardeau Valley and they sent a telegram to their Member of the Legislative Assembly. Within 24 hours, word had spread across the country and rumours flourished about the men, women and children, as well as animals, who were starving in the Lardeau Valley.

Victoria bombarded New Denver with telegrams wondering what was being done about the situation. Someone suggested an airplane be sent in with supplies. Finally, the CPR sent between 40 and 50 men with equipment, a snowplow and a locomotive by barge to Lardeau where they were to attack the snow problem. CPR Divisional Superintendent Sharp went along in his private car.

It took three days to push their way through snow laden with rocks, trees and other debris. And once through, there were delays caused by trees on the rails and the rails tipping because their old ties caused the train to run off the track. They finally arrived at Gerrard only to find that the situation was not as bad as rumour had it.

Sharp opened a boxcar, told the townspeople there was food for them, and asked them to load up their sick for the trip back. When they replied that they were okay and didn't need any help, Sharp, his frustration of the past days getting the better of him, swore loudly, stating that it had cost the railway $35,000 to get the supposedly much-needed supplies to them.

A few years later the line was closed permanently.

If you are in the area on the Canada Day long weekend, stop in to watch the annual Lardeau Valley Relay. It begins at the community hall in Meadow Creek, 12 kilometres (7.5 miles) north of Lardeau. Each team is made up of a runner, two canoeists and a cyclist. The race takes place over 22 kilometres (13.7 miles) with the participants tagging at the end of their relays.

Duncan Dam

Just north of Meadow Creek is the right turn onto the Duncan Dam Observation Point road, which is gravel. You cross the Lardeau River and come to the gates to the dam. You can climb a hill and look down, but continue to the observation point further on. Here you can look out over the dam and the valley with the river flowing through it. A picnic area is under the rows of trees.

Shortly after you turn back onto Highway 31 heading north, you see a large green building on the left. It is Marblehead Station, built in 1898 and now a private residence. Just past the station, the highway becomes gravel. The road is good and you travel along the Lardeau River. At 7 kilometres (4.3 miles) from the Duncan Dam turn-off is the road into Howser, which was a station on the now-closed railway line. Howser Beach and Glayco Beach are both on Duncan Lake, which was formed by the Duncan Dam.

Highway 31 goes through trees, along creeks, across many bridges and past the occasional ranch. Twenty-eight kilometres (17 miles) from Howser, the trees are so close to the road and so tall that the branches almost meet overhead. The Gerrard Provincial Park turn-off is at kilometre 34.1 (mile 21.2). This park is not serviced, so haul your garbage out. There is no well but the Lardeau River flows nearby. And there are toilets.

Just past the park entrance you cross the Lardeau River again and on the other side of the river is another part of the campground. There is also a deck overlooking the river with signs on it explaining about the ghost town of Gerrard.

After the park on Highway 31, a sign warns that you are now on a narrow winding road and to expect heavy industrial logging traffic for the next 27 kilometres (16.7 miles). The Lardeau River flows out of Trout Lake at Gerrard Provincial Park; you are now driving beside the lake and have great views of it and the mountains across it.

TROUT LAKE

At kilometre 25 (mile 15.5), you reach pavement and the hamlet of Trout Lake. Beside the highway is the Trout Lake Store with its two hand-operated gas pumps. Whether you need gas or not, stop in here for the experience.

On the top of the pump sits a glass bowl with each gallon up to 10 measured on it. The owner comes out and pumps the handle until the glass has 10 gallons of gas in it. Then he puts the nozzle into

Trout Lake

your vehicle and lets gravity fill your tank with the amount of gas you need. You can watch as the air bubbles up and the gallons decrease. The store doesn't take credit cards so make sure you have cash to pay for the gas. You can also stock up on groceries here.

Carry on past the store to the road with the Windsor Hotel sign. Turn onto it and you come to the three-storey hotel. It was built in 1892 and has been recently renovated and restored. It rents out rooms, and has a dining room. Across from the hotel are some small cabins. These are known as Little Calgary to the locals, because most of them are owned by people from that city.

THE GRAND OLD LADY OF LARDEAU

Alice Elizabeth Jowett was born in Bradford, Yorkshire, England in 1853. She married in 1878 and was left a widow with four children a few years later. In 1889 she and her children moved to Vancouver where she set up a bakeshop. After seven years she moved to Trout Lake City and opened a small hotel in a log cabin. In 1897, needing more space, she bought the three-storey Windsor Hotel across the street.

Alice Jowett's roast beef and Yorkshire pudding was served on white tablecloths and eaten with silverware. Visitors came from as far away as New York, western Australia and South Africa. One of her famous guests was W.C. Van Horne, president of the CPR.

When bored with the hotel business, she searched the hills on horseback for gold. She staked five claims and leased them out. She made regular trips out to the claims until she was in her late eighties. In 1945, at the age of 92, she flew over her claims to see them from the air. Also at 92, she sold the hotel, retiring from the hotel business after 50 years. She died in Kelowna at the age of 101.

A collection of 22 of this charming lady's garments, in excellent condition, are in the Nakusp Museum.

BONNINGTON BAY TO SANDON

BONNINGTON BAY AND FOUR HOT SPRINGS

Thirteen kilometres (8.1 miles) from Trout Lake on Highway 31 is the turn-off to Bonnington Bay on the northeast arm of Upper Arrow Lake. The road is gravel and steep, but take it to see the bay and a deep, narrow canyon created by a small creek. The drive is about 7 kilometres (4.3 miles) to the bridge over the creek. If the traffic is light, stop on the bridge because that is where you get your best view. Then you drive beside a wider part of the canyon as you continue down to Bonnington Bay. The water of the bay is a bright blue and there is a wide parking area but no tables or toilets. There used to be a town called Beaton near here but it has disappeared (though it still appears on many maps).

Back on Highway 31, at kilometre 17.8 (mile 11.1), is a junction. To the north is Galena Bay. Turn south instead on Highway 23 towards Nakusp. Every road should be travelled twice, once in each direction because the scenery is different. From here to Nakusp you have that opportunity. (See Chapter 8.)

If you wish to soak in a hot springs, set your odometer at the junction and drive for 10.3 kilometres (6.4 miles). You come around a curve and to your right is a white gate across a road. Ahead are two rock walls. To your left is a road that makes a sharp turn and goes immediately uphill and back parallel to the highway. A white sign with red lettering tacked to a tree says 'This is private property. Please do not abuse.' This is the road to the Halcyon Hot Springs. Be prepared for deep holes, but if you drive carefully you can make it.

When the early Natives found these hot springs, they called them 'Great Medicine Waters' and camped beside them for weeks at a time. Sometimes, to maintain possession of the healing waters, they had to do battle with other tribes. Near the end of the 1800s, a tuberculosis sanitarium was build at Halcyon. Patients, as well as tourists, came to relax in the hot springs waters until the buildings burned down. Since then, nothing has been done.

Halfway Hot Springs are further south along Highway 23. Just after you cross the bridge over the Halfway River, take the first left, onto a single-lane, gravel and rock road. When you have gone 10.3 kilometres (6.4 miles), watch to your left for a road that heads down the side of the hill. If you have a four-wheel drive, you will have no problem following this road. Drivers of two-wheelers should drive carefully. This backroad is not recommended for a car, so just park and walk in. If you are pulling a trailer, make sure you have a four-wheel drive mainly for the pull back up.

Bonnington Bay on Upper Arrow Lake

There is a makeshift camping area at the end of this quarter kilometre (sixth of a mile) long road. From here it is a steep walk down the hillside and at the bottom is a giant rock. Past the rock is the springs alongside the Halfway River. There is a square pond plus other natural ponds and hoses to direct the water. It is relaxing to sit in the warm water and watch the river flow by. You can stay at the campsite down there; it is complete with a toilet, but you have to carry your supplies down.

Back on Highway 23 heading south, you cross the next bridge and in 2 kilometres (1.2 miles) is the St. Leon Forest Service Road. It is the first left after the bridge. This gravel road leads to the St. Leon Hot Springs. At kilometre 3.5 (mile 2.2) is a little turnout to the right which will hold about three vehicles. To the left is another steep downhill path. You start with shifting gravel and sand under your feet and then you are onto tree roots. The springs are in a pond shaped like a keyhole and the water is quite hot. The setting is very peaceful down in the tall trees. You can just lay back and relax.

Forty-three kilometres (26.7 miles) south of St. Leon on Highway 23 is the turn-off to the last hot springs on this road, the Nakusp Hot Springs. These ones are developed so the road is

Halfway Hot Springs

paved although narrow and winding. At kilometre 8.5 (mile 5.3) on this road is a sign 'Don't Despair, You're Almost There' and you reach the springs 3 kilometres (1.9 miles) later. There is a parking lot as well as a campground and a picnic and tenting area. Ahead is the rock and cement wall of the hot springs with trees planted on the top.

The waters of the two pools are naturally heated. The larger, cooler pool reaches a temperature of 38°C (100°F) and the smaller, hotter one 41°C (106°F). They are open all year.

NAKUSP

Nakusp Hot Springs

Nakusp was a stop for sternwheelers at the beginning of the century and had a large shipbuilding industry. Fruit orchards were planted in 1906 but during the Depression they couldn't compete with the Okanagan for prices and early delivery dates. In the 1950s, Nakusp became the centre of logging for the Arrow Lakes. It has had steady growth over the years.

To reach the promenade, continue along the highway through the town to the four-way stop. Drive across the road and park to the right. It is just a short walk down to the asphalt walkway along the lakeshore. If you want to relax after the long drive, turn right and go to the Japanese Gardens. There you will find a bench to sit on and enjoy the gardens, Upper Arrow Lake, the hills, and the Selkirk Mountains. It is such a tranquil setting. All along the promenade are benches and flower gardens and you have such great scenery to look at.

Leave Nakusp on Highway 6 heading southeast towards New Denver.

NEW DENVER

As you enter New Denver, watch for the Denver Glacier across Slocan Lake and Idaho Peak above the town. Although New Denver only has a population of 600 now, it was a thriving centre for recording claims during the 1890s silver boom. It was first called Eldorade, but the name was changed because the residents expected its fortunes to be better than those of Denver.

Nikkei Internment Memorial Centre in New Denver

During the Second World War, about 1500 Nikkei (people of Japanese descent) were sent to 'the Orchard,' an internment camp just south of New Denver. Two families had to share a tarpaper shack 4.2 by 8.5 metres (14 by 28 feet). To see New Denver's Nikkei Internment

Memorial Centre, turn south towards Silverton on Highway 6. After you cross Carpenter Creek, watch for 2nd Avenue and turn right, go two blocks and turn right again. There are signs posted.

A guided walk through the centre will acquaint you with the living conditions of the Japanese Canadians during the war. The Peace Arch is a replica of the 1945 one that had been built to symbolize peace and harmony among all humans. There is also a Japanese garden and tarpaper shacks that were moved from their original site to the centre.

This centre was created by the Kyowakai ('working together peacefully') Society, which is the only remaining internment camp organization in operation.

JAPANESE INTERNMENT

In 1942, during the Second World War, the federal government, fearing a breach of security by the Japanese people in Canada, moved 22,000 Nikkei from their homes. Although 75% were Canadian citizens, all were labelled enemy aliens and their civil rights were taken away. They were gathered together in Hastings Park in Vancouver and moved to camps in the interior of British Columbia and to sugar beet farms in Alberta, Manitoba and Ontario. In 1994, Anne Wheeler directed a film, The War Between Us, *about this period in Canada's history. It was actually filmed in New Denver, though the story takes place in Slocan.*

Highway 31A east of New Denver will take you to the historic town of Sandon, a must to see. About 25 people live there now and the town is in the process of being restored.

At kilometre 8 (mile 5) is a Y in the road: left is to Kaslo, right a gravel road following Carpenter Creek towards Sandon. The town bills itself as 'The City of Sandon, 1898–1920.' As you turn into it and drive across the bridge over Carpenter Creek, on your left you will see some old foundations. These ruins are what is left of the powerhouse. It was built in 1896, making it BC's first hydro-electric facility.

Prospector's Pick is a little shop and tourist information in the basement of City Hall. You can pick up arts, crafts, books and postcards. There are also displays in an antique china cabinet, an old piano and old wood stove. The upper two storeys of City Hall are being restored.

Sandon City Hall

For a dollar you can buy a map of the town to use on your walking tour. Part of the proceeds from the sales of this or any other item go towards restoring the town. An amazing number of old buildings are still standing. You pass the museum in the old mercantile building, go up one street, and cross the creek to another street. Main street ran between the buildings and Carpenter Creek so to see the fronts of the City Hall building and the museum you have to stand by the creek.

Sandon was incorporated as a city in 1898 with a population of 5000 and 2000 in the outlying area. It had 24 hotels, 23 saloons, two railways and 115 ladies in its red light district.

In 1899 the first legally registered union in BC was organized by the miners who were tired of the poor living and working conditions. The union held a six-month strike in 1899. However, the metal prices fell and many of the residents left to join the Klondike Gold Rush. On May 4, 1900 a fire broke out in the opera house and quickly spread down the tightly packed, wooden buildings along the streets. By the time it was over, it had destroyed most of the business section, causing over $750,000 in damage and losses. Although much of the town was rebuilt and it survived the flood of 1901, people were moving out. In 1920 the city went bankrupt and was disincorporated.

There was a short, small revival in 1923 and again during the war with the internment of 4000 Japanese Canadian people. But the flood of 1955 was the final blow to the town, although the post office remained open until 1962. There is still a mine working in Sandon. It is the Dickenson Mine in the big white and silver building you see across the creek as you arrive at the town.

Old mining equipment in Sandon

To reach Idaho Peak, go past City Hall and at the museum turn right and follow the road. It is a steep, winding, narrow road; you should have a truck to attempt it. This road is one of only a handful in the province that come out above the tree line into an alpine meadow. Along the way you pass many of the old mines, and at the top you will be on the Silver Ridge of the 2280 metre (7480 foot) Idaho Mountain. From here it is a short walk to the lookout. The 12 kilometre (7.5 mile) road is usually closed until mid-June, so check the road conditions before going.

Back at Highway 31A you can head east to Kaslo or west back to New Denver and continue south. If you go east you pass more ghost towns from the silver boom era.

When you get back into New Denver, at the flashing light you turn left onto Highway 6. You follow the Slocan Lake shore as you travel south. To the west across the lake are the Valhalla Mountains.

SILVERTON TO SLOCAN VALLEY

SILVERTON

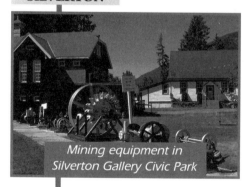
Mining equipment in Silverton Gallery Civic Park

Silverton is south of New Denver. The Silverton Museum is unusual in that it is outside. Just after you cross Silverton Creek, watch for it on your right in the Silverton Gallery Civic Park. Lining the sidewalks up to the gallery are pieces of mining equipment all restored and painted.

The Silverton Hotel was established in 1897. It is a lovely building of historic beauty that has been refurbished and still rents out

Silverton Hotel

rooms. It is on the left side of the main street as you drive through town. Take a look at the pilings in the water where the sternwheelers docked to load ore during the boom.

SLOCAN AND THE SLOCAN VALLEY

Slocan once had a population of 6000, but now is only one-tenth the size. It bills itself as the smallest incorporated city in the world.

The Silvery Slocan country yielded millions of dollars in silver from such mines as the Slocan Star, Last Chance, Enterprise and Rambler-Cariboo. More than 12,000 men were involved with silver mining and thousands more in other necessary occupations. The silver ore was ferried from the mines around New Denver to the railhead at Slocan City by paddlewheelers. Eventually, as with all the mining history, the ore ran out and the boom died.

South from Slocan on Highway 6 you travel through many small towns, some of which seem to run together. There are valleys with farmland, rivers and creeks, and mountains. At kilometre 46 (mile 28.5) is the junction with Highway 3A. Turn right towards Castlegar. Fourteen kilometres (8.7 miles) from the junction is a rest area with a Silvery Slocan historic sign. Stop and read the sign about the history of this valley. South of here is Castlegar.

LOST SILVER

In 1904, the Consolidated Mining and Smelting Company sent a boxcar load of silver bars across Slocan Lake by barge. A storm came up and the barge began rolling with the waves. The boxcar also began rolling on its track and on one big wave, smashed through the railing of the barge and disappeared over the edge.

Soundings showed that the boxcar was in about 30 metres (100 feet) of water and lying on a steep slope. It could be dislodged by water currents or salvage attempts. The men in charge decided to raise the whole car rather than try to remove the silver bars. Divers rigged the car to the barge. The crew up top slowly began winching in the cable.

Finally the car rose above the surface and the men rushed to guide another barge under it. But a cable snapped. The boxcar hit the barge and once more slipped under the murky waters of Slocan Lake. Divers went down again and reported that the car had broken in two and the silver was buried in the muddy bottom.

During the Depression, an attempt was made to recover the bullion. A diver went down and after looking at the boxcar decided that the silver was still in one side of it. He carefully began digging through the silt and pulled up something solid which he sent to the top. It was a silver ingot. He kept groping and sending up bars, until fear that the car might shift and kill him made him stop. However, he did manage to retrieve over 20 silver bars before quitting.

In the years since, the railway car has moved with the changing of the lake bottom and the silver has disappeared into the mud.

CHAPTER 7
CHRISTINA LAKE TO KELOWNA

On the way to Grand Forks

CHRISTINA LAKE TO KELOWNA

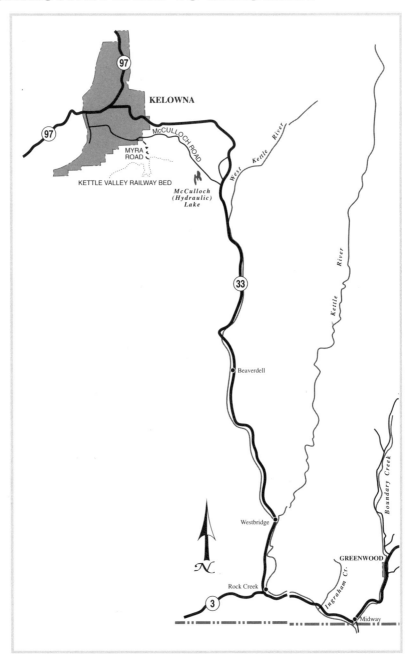

> **This route is not long but it is historic. You begin by driving on much of the old Dewdney Trail and when you swing north, you follow the Kettle Valley Railway (KVR) route. At the end, you can enjoy a long walk on a piece of history.**

CHRISTINA LAKE TO GRAND FORKS

CHRISTINA LAKE

Christina Lake is southwest of Castlegar on Highway 3. It is claimed to be the warmest lake in BC for swimming. Its waters have an average summer temperature of 22.7°C (73°F). On the east end of the lake is Texas Creek Provincial Park. If you have a boat, go along the shore of the park and look for the Native pictographs on the rocks. There are a number of these pictographs throughout the province, but owing to vandalism their exact whereabouts is being kept a secret. The ones here can only be seen from a boat.

The resort town of Christina Lake is spread along the lakeshore and has ice cream stands, fruit stands, boat rentals, camping and boat launches.

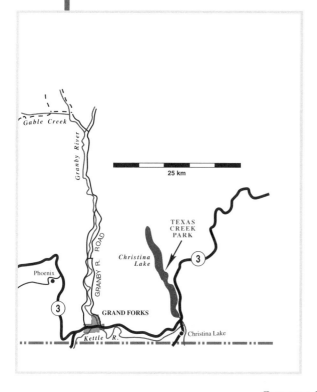

On the way to Grand Forks

Leave Christina Lake behind and travel on Highway 3 through the Kettle Valley and beside the Kettle River. In the summertime, the treed region gives way to wide open areas, rock outcroppings and brown grass. The countryside is very rugged and dry, and the closer you get to Grand Forks the more rugged it is.

GRAND FORKS

Grand Forks is near the border with the USA, at the confluence of the Kettle and Granby rivers (hence its name). Both these rivers are ideal for canoeing and kayaking. The town is famous for sunshine and borscht. Most restaurants offer authentic Doukhobor food.

The Boundary Museum and tourist information are at the Chamber of Commerce building on 5th Street. Outside the museum is Gyro Park and some antique firefighting equipment enclosed in shelters. The Steam Pumper was built in 1901 and purchased July 19, 1920 for $1600. It pumped over 3400 litres (750 gallons) of water per minute and is fired by coal. Beside it is the town's original fire bell, first used in 1896.

Inside the museum is a gift shop and a collection of maps dating back to 1896. They show old fur-trade routes, the railways and mines, and early settlements. Anyone into photography will want to see the photo gallery with pictures and images dating from 1897.

GRANBY ROAD

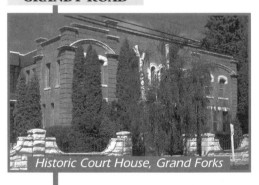
Historic Court House, Grand Forks

For a backroad experience, take the Granby River Road (#221) north of town. As you enter Grand Forks, at the Omega Restaurant instead of following Highway 3 to the left into town take the road ahead that runs beside the restaurant. You pass through a couple of blocks of residences then you are out of town on a paved road.

The Pumper in Gyro Park, Grand Forks

Granby Road is on part of the Kettle Valley Railway bed, which went up to Lynch Creek. The scenery is very different through here: not really mountain country, it is more like big rock country. The scenery varies from trees to open areas, valleys to hills and grassland to rock.

When you come to the yield sign at kilometre 15.5 (mile 9.6) turn to the right if you want to continue the journey through this ever-changing country. If you want to make the circle tour back to Grand Forks and Highway 3, continue straight ahead and cross the bridge. (Older maps may suggest going straight here to continue and a left turn to return to Grand Forks.)

At kilometre 27.4 (mile 17) you reach a cattleguard and the end of pavement. You turn to your left here and cross a wooden bridge. On the left is the Granby/Burrell Recreation Site with picnic tables. You can climb a slight ridge and have a great view of the Granby River.

This place is lovely and peaceful. After lunch you can decide if you are going to continue ahead or turn back. The roads are not paved but there are many picnic sites and primitive camping areas.

If you wish to go to Greenwood by a backroad, continue up the Granby Road for 6.5 kilometres (4 miles) then turn left onto Gable Creek Road. In 0.5 kilometres (0.3 miles) you will come to a picnic site, which is RV accessible. Continue along Gable Creek Road to Boundary Creek Road and turn left. This road will take you to Greenwood.

Doukhobor Museum in Grand Forks

If you return the same way you came, when you reach the yield sign follow to the right and you will cross the 10 Mile Bridge. You are now on the North Fork Road. At kilometre 14.6 (mile 9) watch for Harding Road. Turn right and follow it up to the Doukhobor Museum. From there you will have a panoramic view of the hills, Grand Forks and the Sunshine Valley, as it is called.

At kilometre 16 (mile 10) you come to a stop sign and Highway 3.

GREENWOOD TO MIDWAY

GREENWOOD

Greenwood Hotel

With a population of less than 1000, Greenwood is one of the smallest incorporated cities in Canada. Built along Boundary Creek, it began in 1895 as a central town for the mining camps. In 1897 the town was incorporated as a city and the population reached 3000 by 1899. Also in that year, the BC Copper Company built a smelter to process the ore from the Mother Lode Mine and the Columbia and Western Railway reached the town. At the end of the First World War, the demand for copper and the supply of copper both dwindled. During the Second World War, about 1200 Japanese Canadians were interned in the old buildings. After the war, mining was revived for a few years but now the city relies on logging.

MOTHER LODE

Although nothing was done about the Mother Lode until 1896, the copper outcropping was discovered and staked in 1891. The surface ore was mined from six quarries and eventually formed a giant 'glory hole.' In 1909 the Mother Lode set a record by mining 349,350 tonnes (385,085 tons). But then it was decided that the glory hole should be made bigger immediately.

In August 1913, 4834 holes were driven in the rock and filled with 22,475 kilograms (49,548 pounds) of 40% powder. Forty holes were wired in each group and 26,532 metres (87,047 feet) of electric wire joined them together. As a precaution, three safety switches were set on the circuit so it couldn't go off accidentally.

Everyone was sent off the hill and the switches were flicked. After the noise and dust had settled, approximately 39,000 tonnes (42,989 tons) of ore had been blasted apart. However, the low-grade ore was contaminated with waste and the mine was found to be hazardous. The edge of the 'glory hole' collapsed, covering some of the chutes used to remove the ore. The Mother Lode era was over.

"Hell's bells" in Lotzkar Memorial Park

To get to the old smelter site at Lotzkar Memorial Park, follow Highway 3 as it curves west through Greenwood to the Motherlode Store on your right just past the service station. Turn right, cross the bridge, go past the house and yard, and turn in at the first left.

You start to see smelter ruins and lots of waste slag as you enter Lotzkar park. This slag was brought here from the smelter in bell-shaped slag cars. It was dumped out as a molten clump of black glass and glowed red until the temperature died down. The black 'bowls' lying on the ground – called 'hell's bells' – were used to transport the slag here.

Look up and you will see the smokestack from the smelter. You can walk up to the stack or you can drive to it. To drive, go back to the house, which is a heritage site, and take the rock road to the left. The road meets up with the pavement from the Motherlode Store. Once on the pavement, you climb a hill. At the top, turn left. You have a great view of the valley below and then you reach the smokestack. From here you can look down at Lotzkar Park.

If the fence is open, walk into the stack. Look up and see the sky through the opening in the top. Yell and listen to the echo. Look down the hill and see the flume. It used to be enclosed but its top has slowly fallen in. The miners would stoke up the fire down the hill and the smoke would come up the flume and out the stack. The stack is 36 metres (118 feet) tall, made from 250,000 bricks, and was the highest stack in BC when it was built.

Smoke stack, Greenwood

Looking down the flume of the smelter, Greenwood

The smelter, constructed at the mouth of Copper Creek in 1898, was described as the most complete and modern in the world. The blowing of the first furnace occurred on February 18, 1901 and the smelter ran 24 hours a day. It only operated for 17 years, finally closing on November 26, 1918 owing to shortages of ore. The original sheet metal smokestack was replaced in 1904 by this brick one.

If you want to see the Mother Lode Mine itself, starting back at the Motherlode store on the paved road, turn left and you will be on gravel. In 2.4 kilometres (1.5 miles) you reach the Motherlode Road with a sign. Then you come to a T intersection. Turn left and you get to the mine site in about 4.8 kilometres (3 miles). Stay on the road and view the site from there, because the open pits are dangerous and are on private property.

Five kilometres (3 miles) from Greenwood is a point of interest with a plaque describing the Dewdney Trail, which Highway 3 follows for most of its length.

Cairn along Dewdney Trail

PHOENIX

At an elevation of 1400 metres (4595 feet) Phoenix was the highest city in Canada, and for a while it was the largest producer of copper ore. It was built on a mountain of copper and became a city in 1900. By 1911, 4000 people lived there.

It was a prosperous place with tennis courts, moving pictures, curling and hockey. In fact, the first professional hockey game in British Columbia was played on the hockey rink in Phoenix.

Because the city was built on copper, some of the mining was done under the buildings. Occasionally, a cave-in would leave railway tracks hanging in mid-air and buildings teetering precariously.

The mine was closed in 1919 and the residents quickly moved to other work, leaving the buildings. Within a year Phoenix was a ghost town. In 1955 the mining company returned and developed an open-pit mine. It soon had eaten up the old town site and all that remains is the old cemetery.

MIDWAY

Follow Highway 3 west from Greenwood to Midway, in the beautiful Kettle Valley. It is the oldest town site in the Boundary area. Its first resident arrived in 1884 and began ranching. It was first known as Eholts and changed to Boundary City when lots were sold in 1893.

There are two stories as to why its name was changed to Midway. One is that a man from Montreal, who had attended the Chicago World Fair in 1893 and had been impressed with its 'midway,' sug-

Kettle Valley Railway Museum at Midway

gested the name be changed. Another is that the town is halfway between the West Coast and the Rockies. Whatever the reason, the name was changed to Midway on November 1, 1894.

July 5, 1910 marked the beginning of construction of the Kettle Valley Railway. In late 1912 the long, arduous 331.5 kilometre (206 mile) route between Midway and Princeton had been completed. (It is only 128.7 kilometres [80 miles] in a direct line from Midway to Princeton.) In that year the tracks from Merritt to Brookmere were also laid. In 1913, the CPR took over the railway and passenger service began on May 31, 1915 from Midway to Merritt to the Fraser Canyon and on to Vancouver.

To see the Kettle Valley Railway Museum at Midway, stay on Highway 3 past the turn-off into town. The museum is on the right-hand side along the highway.

Just out of Midway you must slow down to 40 kilometres (25 miles) an hour in order to make a 90° turn to your right and then another curve to your left.

BOUNDARY COUNTRY

The area between Christina Lake and Midway is known as Boundary Country. It is believed that the first non-Native to travel through this region was the famous botanist David Douglas, for whom the Douglas-fir is named.

The Oregon Treaty of 1846 set the border at the 49th parallel, but it made little difference to the people and economy of the area. Trails still carried people from Washington to the Okanagan. Hunters on either side still hunted and cattle were grazed wherever. The area became known as Boundary Country or just plain Boundary.

ROCK CREEK TO KELOWNA

ROCK CREEK

At Rock Creek, west of Midway on Highway 3, turn north onto Highway 33 to go to Kelowna. This road is shorter, more scenic and less hectic than the Osoyoos to Kelowna route, and it has some wonderful history. It follows the old Kettle Valley Railway line although you won't see much of it.

Just after the turn is Prospector's Pub. The original Prospector's Pub was built in 1895. The building has been renovated and redone a number of times but part of the original pub still remains.

Beaverdell Hotel

Placer gold was discovered on Rock Creek, a tributary of the Kettle River, in 1859. By June of 1860, $83,000 worth of gold (in 1860 dollars) had been recovered. This was the beginning of the search for minerals in Boundary Country. Rock Creek also became the terminus of the Dewdney Trail built in 1861 from New Westminster.

WESTBRIDGE AND BEAVERDELL

The town of Westbridge is off Highway 33, but there is a service station and grocery store on the highway.

A nice canoe trip is down the Kettle River from here to where the Ingraham Creek bridge crosses the river about 4 kilometres (2.5 miles) past the town of Rock Creek. The river is Grade I with some rapids making it a Grade II. During high water, it could go up to a Grade III. (See p.51 for an explanation of river grades.) If you go further to where a bridge crosses the river at Midway, you will have a 30 metre (100 foot) portage around a spillway about 10 kilometres (6 miles) downstream. Watch for the signs.

Beaverdell Hotel, on the main street of Beaverdell, was built before 1900. It is one of the oldest hotels in the province and once featured a ladies' parlour.

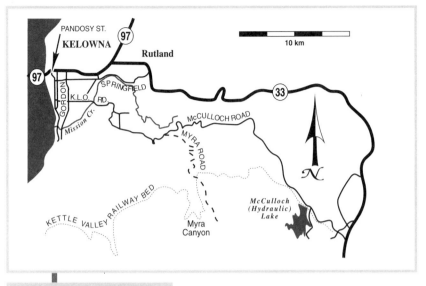

MCCULLOCH ROAD

To hike on part of the old Kettle Valley Railway bed and over some trestles, watch for the Idabell Lake Resort and McCulloch Lake Resort signs at kilometre 40 (mile 24.9) from Beaverdell. Turn left onto McCulloch Road.

You pass both resorts and follow McCulloch Road for 26.3 kilometres (16.3 miles). That hill to your right with striped layers of

Cycling along the Kettle Valley Railway

rock almost like steps is called Layer Cake Hill. At times you will be able to see the highway across the valley and Kelowna.

At kilometre 24.6 (mile 15.3) on the McCulloch Road, you cross a cattleguard and come to a Y intersection. Go to the right. Near the end the road widens, has some washboard, and there are a couple houses. When you see these houses, start watching for the Myra Road sign. It is at kilometre 26.3 (mile 16.3) but is turned slightly in the other direction so might be hard to see.

A tunnel on the Kettle Valley Railway

Myra Forest Service Road climbs, and is washboardy and narrow. At kilometre 8.5 (mile 5.3) you reach a crossroads with the old railway bed. There is a sign that says 'Trestles' with an arrow pointing right. In about 0.5 kilometre (0.3 mile) you reach the parking lot.

The Kettle Valley Railway came north from Midway, turned west to pass by Hydraulic Lake, now known as McCulloch Lake, and hugged the hills to Chute Lake. Here it made a steep descent to Naramata, between Peachland and Penticton on #147, using a spiral tunnel.

Andrew McCulloch, in charge of laying the tracks, was horrified when he saw the hillside route the railway was to take. But instead of taking the longer and more costly route along the Okanagan lakeshore, he built 16 wooden trestles and two steel ones, and blasted two tunnels through the rock to complete the line.

Don't let the beginning scare you off. That is the only bad part. The rest is an excellent, well-kept trail. You are walking on the

Entering a tunnel on the Kettle Valley Railway

One of the trestles on the Kettle Valley Railway

railway bed sometimes through trees, sometimes with the Myra Canyon to your right, sometimes between rock walls. The first trestle you reach is number 18. They are all numbered and a plaque beside each one tells who donated money or time to fixing each one up. All the trestles have boards nailed onto the timbers for a walkway and railings put up so that no one falls off.

It is a great walk along the canyon edge. You can see out over the valley to Kelowna. Across the canyon you can see other trestles hugging the side of the mountain and the long one that spans the canyon.

When you reach the tunnels, be careful of rock falling from the ceiling. The wind whips through these tunnels so expect to be chilly. Watch for bikers and joggers. You can walk as far as you want or make it an all-day hike from number 18 to number 1 and back. On an overcast day bring along an extra jacket. It gets cool along the canyon edge.

If you decide to carry on down Highway 33 instead of turning onto McCulloch Road, you will reach Rock Creek Summit (elevation 1265 metres [4150 feet]) in a few kilometres and Kelowna in about 25 kilometres (15.5 miles).

CHAPTER 8
COLDSTREAM TO REVELSTOKE

Galena Bay/Shelter Bay Ferry over Upper Arrow Lake

COLDSTREAM TO REVELSTOKE

On this trip, you cross the Arrow Lakes twice on
ferries, see two waterfalls, visit three dams and
stop in at four hot springs. The scenery is very
impressive, so linger awhile and relax on the drive.

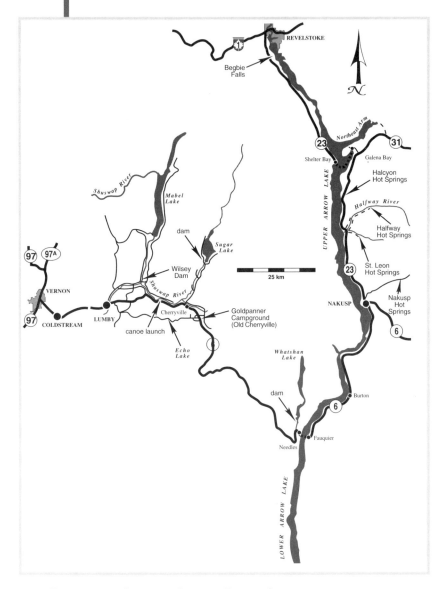

COLDSTREAM TO NEEDLES

COLDSTREAM

Coldstream is a district, not a town, and its inhabitants say it is rural living at its best. As you come east out of Vernon on Highway 6 into Coldstream, there are orchards, irrigation and crops along the highway with hills in the background.

At kilometre 3.5 (mile 2.2) from the 'Welcome to Coldstream' sign, you begin a sharp S curve, cross railway tracks and come to Coldstream Ranch Limited. In the 1860s, George Forbes Vernon and his brother started a ranch in the Coldstream Valley. In 1861, Lord Aberdeen planted the first orchard in the Vernon area. After he became Governor General of Canada, he bought the Coldstream Ranch from the Vernon brothers. He built it into one of the best fruit producers in the British Empire. It eventually grew into one of the largest ranches in Canada.

Coldstream Ranch now includes about 2950 hectares (7300 acres) and has hundreds more deeded and leased. Other ranches have become historic sites, but this one is still a working ranch. Over the years it has diversified into orchards, farming and growing corn.

LUMBY

Lumby Days are held the first weekend of June. Lumby is known as 'the Gateway to the Monashees.' *Monashee* is a Gaelic word meaning 'mountains and peace.'

To get to the Wilsey Dam at Shuswap Falls, take the Mabel Lake Road at the flashing light in Lumby. At about 16 kilometres (10 miles) you cross a bridge over the Shuswap River. Turn left after the bridge and into the Wilsey Dam/Shuswap Falls Recreation Area.

From the viewpoint, you get a great view of the water tumbling down from your left, churning in front, and plunging over the spillway channel. The Wilsey Dam and 3 megawatt (4000 horsepower) generating station were built in 1929 on the original site of the Shuswap Falls. There was no water storage until 1942 when a dam was constructed at the outlet of Sugar Lake. This dam created a storage capacity of 15,400 hectare-metres (125,000 acre-feet) between elevations 591 metres (1939 feet) and 602 metres (1975 feet). That's about 154 million cubic metres (5.5 billion cubic feet) of water.

On your way eastwards out of Lumby on Highway 6, if you want to try honey with a twist, stop in at the Specialty Honey Products. To get there, after you cross the bridge over Harris Creek, turn to your right, go down to Dyffryn Road, and turn left. Specialty Honey is at the end of the road. The apiarists in the area spent months blending different fruits with their honey to get the right taste. They now have eight different Honey and Fruit Spreads.

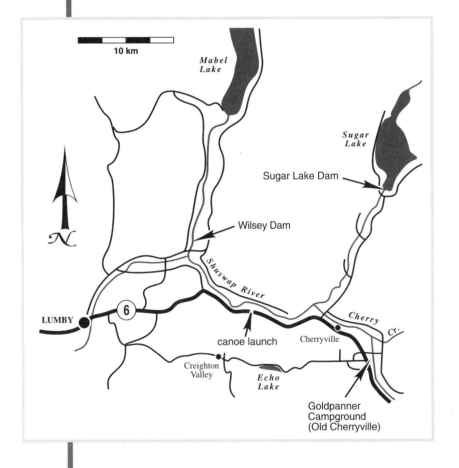

THE HUMP TOUR

That mountain you see as you leave Lumby is the Camel's Hump or 'The Hump' as the locals call it. If you want to take a different road to Cherryville, stop in at the Lumby Tourist Information building and pick up a map for the tour around the south side of The Hump. You turn on Creighton Valley Road just east of Lumby and follow it through an interior rainforest, a dry interior grassland, and past Echo Lake before reaching Cherryville.

After great success with that, they branched out into Honey and Liqueurs. They also began manufacturing six Specialty Honey Mustards and are now the only federally approved mustard manufacturing plant in western Canada. At their store, you can look through a window and watch the preparation process. They are open from 10 am to 5 pm, and tours are offered that include a visit to a tasting room and an observation hive.

At kilometre 24.4 (mile 15.2) you reach the Shuswap River Recreation Area and Canoe Launch. The Shuswap River has its source in the Monashee Mountains and in the spring can be quite high. It feeds Sugar Lake, runs through the dam, then flows past here on the 37 kilometre (23 mile) journey to Wilsey Dam. From there it goes north to Mabel Lake then on to Shuswap Lake.

Specialty Honey Products at Lumby

Canoe launch
on Shuswap River

To get your canoe down to the river you carry it past the recreation sign to the trail into the trees. It is only about a quarter of a kilometre (a sixth of a mile) walk. You can carry your picnic lunch down here and eat at one of the tables by the river. If the water is low enough, you can swim by the shore.

At kilometre 8 (mile 5) from the canoe launch, you come to a service station and the turn towards Sugar Lake Dam. The dam is about 15 kilometres (9.3 miles) north along the paved and gravel road.

From the viewpoint you can see the dam and the water churning below. Beside the dam is an open area, which is also used as a picnic site. To reach it, get back on the road and drive down the hill. You will cross a one-lane wooden bridge over the Shuswap River. To your left is a trail into the trees, or you can go further and take the next left. On this road take the left when you come to a Y intersection.

Sugar Lake Dam is at Brenda Falls. It is 13 metres (42.6 feet) high and 102 metres (334.6 feet) long. Sugar Lake is fed by the Shuswap River and is part of the north Okanagan. The most commonly found fish species include kokanee, whitefish, Dolly Varden and rainbow and Kamloops trout.

CHERRYVILLE AND NEEDLES

About 2.5 kilometres (1.5 miles) from the service station is a paved road to the left. It is the road into the hamlet of Cherryville, which holds Cherryville Days the weekend after Lumby Days.

If you have a craving for baked goods, stop in at Kirsten's Bakery, 6.5 kilometres (4 miles) along Highway 6 from Cherryville. Kirsten makes bread, cinnamon buns, carrot cake, squares, cookies, cakes and strudels. The bakery is also a coffee shop so you can sit and enjoy your treat but you have to get there early because it sells out fast. Ask for Kirsten's special menu.

People searching for the elusive metal called gold can stop in at the Goldpanner Cafe and Campground at kilometre 9 (mile 5.6). You can pan here for a small fee, and if you forgot your pan you can rent one. Panning is free for campers. You can get gravel from the

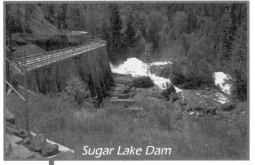
Sugar Lake Dam

office or go down to the Monashee Creek and try your luck there. Lessons in gold panning are available if you have never tried it before.

The campground is open in March and stays open until freeze-up. The cafe is open year-round. There is a gift shop and in the yard is a mining museum and an old miner's cabin. The BC Open Gold Panning Competition is held here on the Victoria Day weekend in May. Even if you don't enter, it is fun watching. If the Goldpanner Campground is full, just a few kilometres (2 or 3 miles) down the road is Fiddlesticks, which offers the same fun.

The actual original site of Cherryville is about 3.5 kilometres (2 miles) through the bush from the Goldpanner Campground. Old Cherryville was founded in the 1860s by prospectors who had left the California gold rush. Its fame came from the ore in the area, which assayed out at between $1500 and $2000 a ton (in 1860s dollars). There was better than 16 kilograms (570 ounces) of silver and 56 grams (2 ounces) of gold per ton. In 1867 a silver-laden rock of 68 kilograms (150 pounds) was blasted from a 1 metre (3 foot) thick ledge that had been found by the Cherry Creek Company.

Then death, legal problems and news that the mine had run out threw the area into oblivion until mid-1876. In that year three companies of miners began working above the old Cherry Creek Silver Mine property. Both gold and silver were found in enough quantities to keep the miners looking until the early 1890s.

Goldpanner Campground

No one knows where the name Cherry Creek came from, as there wasn't a cherry tree in the valley. There were, however, choke-cherry bushes. The budding prospector might be interested in knowing that the mother-lode in this area was never found.

GOLD IS WHERE YOU FIND IT

Gold moves. As the waters flow over the mother-lode, which is usually high up in the mountains, flakes continually wear off and are transported downstream. Gold is four to six times heavier than the river gravel so it will settle out of the rushing water quickly. It is usually deposited on the inside of curves in the rivers, behind rocks or obstructions that slow down the water flow, in tree roots, and at the base of waterfalls. Gold is slightly heavier than black sand so where black sand has settled there could be gold.

Beware of iron pyrite or fool's gold. Iron pyrite looks like gold in the sun but loses its luster in the shade. Gold will appear very much the same in the shade as in the sun. Iron pyrite is also hard and brittle and will shatter easily. Gold is soft and will dent or bend rather than break.

Because of its softness, gold can be twisted, squeezed or rolled into different shapes. It can be pounded so fine it can be seen through and still remain a solid sheet. An ounce of pure gold can be drawn so thin that it will stretch for 56 kilometres (35 miles) without breaking.

The Monashee Summit is 36 kilometres (22.4 miles) east of Cherryville. It has an elevation of 1241 metres (4072 feet).

The bridge across the Whatshan River is about 80 kilometres (50 miles) from Cherryville and just after the crossing take the first turn to your left. Once you are off the highway and onto the road, it splits. Go to the second road and turn left. At kilometre 2.8 (mile 1.7) from the highway, you reach the turn-off to the dam. If you go too far, you will come to overhead power lines across the road. Turn around and go back to the third road and turn left and this will take you the short distance in to the dam.

Goldpanner Campground

This dam is different: whereas the other two had water rushing through their spillways, this one has grass and weeds growing in its spillway. It doesn't look like it's been used in a few years. It is a nice secluded spot on the lake here if you want to have a picnic, but there are no tables. There is a campground past those power lines. At Whatshan Lake you

Whatshan Dam

can fish for rainbow trout and Dolly Varden. Fly-fishing is good to July 15 and trolling for Dolly Varden could net you one up to 4.5 kilograms (10 pounds).

Back on the highway, it is downhill to Needles and the ferry. The ferry runs every half hour between 5:15 am and 9:45 pm and the ride takes about five minutes. Here, Lower Arrow Lake looks emerald green.

FAUQUIER TO REVELSTOKE

FAUQUIER AND BURTON

Ferry over Lower Arrow Lake

On the other side of the lake is Fauquier, which has all the usual tourist services. For a tasty delight, visit the Mushroom Addition Restaurant. Here you will find a selection of dishes that feature wild mushrooms grown in the area.

At kilometre 20.8 (mile 13) from Fauquier you cross a bridge, with the lake to your left and a small pond to the right. You can park at the end of the bridge and fish off it. Just a short ways from the bridge is a cairn that commemorates the community of Burton and its former residents, who are buried in a cemetery near this location. Burton consists of a few houses and a service station.

NAKUSP, GALENA BAY AND SHELTER BAY

Every road should be driven twice, once each way, because the scenery is different from each direction. The road from here to Galena Bay is one that you get to travel twice, south in Chapter 6 and north in this chapter. (For your convenience, the section already covered in Chapter 6 is described here again with the direction reversed.)

Naskusp Japanese on Promenade

The first town after the ferry, Nakusp, has a promenade along the lake shore. Just north of town on Highway 23 is the Nakusp Hot Springs road; the springs are 11.5 km (7.1 miles) from the highway.

Nineteen kilometres (11.8 miles) from Nakusp is a rest area with a falls on the right. Go 2.1 kilometres (1.3 miles) past the rest area to the first road to the right. A sign says 'St. Leon Forest Service Road.' St. Leon Hot Springs is 3.5 kilometres (2.2 miles) down this gravel road.

At kilometre 1.6 (mile 1) down Highway 23 from this forest service road is a bridge and just past it is another road to the right. If you get to the second bridge, you have gone too far. This single-lane gravel road will take you to Halfway Hot Springs in 10.3 kilometres (6.4 miles).

Back on Highway 23 you cross the Halfway River. At kilometre 10.1 (6.3 miles) from the river you will drive between two rock walls and see a gravel road at a V angle to the highway to the right. A white sign nailed to a tree states in red lettering 'This is private property. Please do not abuse.' Follow the rough gravel road in to Halcyon Hot Springs. Remember that this site is not serviced, so take your garbage out with you.

About 10 kilometres (6 miles) from Halcyon Hot Springs is the junction with Highway 31, which goes past Trout Lake. Two kilometres (1.2 miles) past the junction is Galena Bay and the ferry. The ferries are free because they are part of the road system. At Galena Bay there is just a rest area, but no services.

At Shelter Bay there is rock on both sides of the ferry dock. The Arrow Lake Provincial Park is to your right just after you get off the ferry. As you head north, you will be driving between the Selkirk Mountains to the east and the Monashee Mountains to the west.

When you reach Mulvehill Creek at kilometre 28.7 (mile 17.8), look to your left as you cross. There is a slender, deep, deep canyon. Because of its narrowness you have to look quickly or you miss it.

St. Leon Hot Springs

The creek is a long ways below you as it flows towards Upper Arrow Lake to your right.

Watch for the small sign for Mount Begbie Road at kilometre 46.6 (mile 29). Turn right onto the road. It is paved and you will round a curve and come to another small sign that says Begbie Falls. Just past that sign at kilometre 2.2 (mile 1.3) you will reach gravel. At kilometre 4.1 (mile 2.5) you will come to a Y intersection; take the right fork. It is a rough, narrow road, but the tree branches meet overhead so it is a beautiful, shady, peaceful drive.

Natural pool at Halfway Hot Springs

You reach the Begbie Falls Recreation Site 6.5 kilometres (4 miles) from the highway. Here there are two paths to go to the falls. The one beside the sign will take you to where you can watch the river come down out of the hills from the right and curve around in front of you. You can hear it going over the falls to your left.

Galena Bay Ferry over Upper Arrow Lake

The other trail to the left of the picnic area will take you right down to the viewing stand at the base of falls. The trail is steep, but squared timbers have been put in to make steps in the worst parts. The waterfall is not very high but it is divided by an outcropping of rock making it into two separate falls.

From the turn-off to the falls, it is about 3 kilometres (2 miles) down the highway to the outskirts of Revelstoke.

SIR MATTHEW BAILLIE BEGBIE

Matthew Begbie was born at the Cape of Good Hope, South Africa, on May 9, 1819. In 1858 he became the first judge of the new colony of British Columbia. He was a hard but fair judge throughout the mining camps and worked at making sure British Columbia remained British in spite of the majority of American miners living here. When BC entered confederation in 1871, Begbie was appointed its first justice.

Mount Begbie Falls

CHAPTER 9
ENDERBY TO OSOYOOS

Gas pump at Nahun on Westside Road

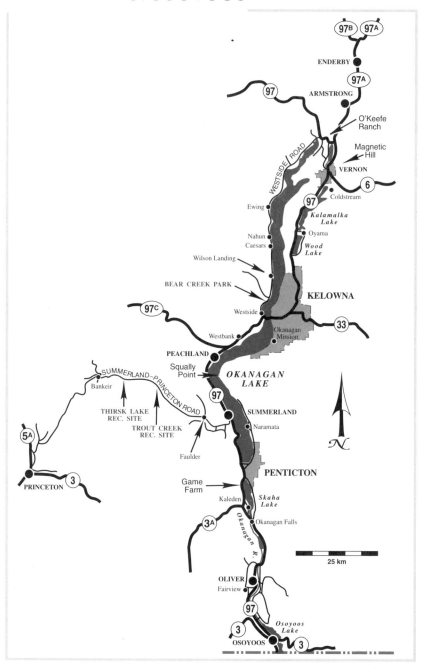

Hundreds of orchards, fruit stands and packing houses are along this road. There are fruit and juice processors, fruit snacks producers, jam and jelly producers, and wine makers. You can stop and purchase any of their products or do a wine sampling tour by watching for the signs with the bunch of purple grapes.

In spite of the green you see as you travel this road, the Okanagan Valley is arid and the southern part is a desert. Away from the irrigation you will find sagebrush, cactus and greasewood.

ENDERBY TO KELOWNA

ENDERBY AND ARMSTRONG

Enderby is situated along Highway 97A, at the northern tip of the Okanagan Valley. Towering above the town to the east are the volcanic Enderby Cliffs. On your way south through the town, watch for the Lions Club campground, with its outdoor swimming pool, if you want to camp or swim.

As you near Armstrong the number of orchards increases. In 1892, at the completion of the Shuswap/Okanagan Railway, Armstrong consisted of a single boxcar that housed the ticket office and the rail agent. Now it is a fair-sized town.

To visit the Armstrong Cheese Factory, watch for the 'Armstrong Cheese' sign as you come into town and turn right. When you go through the stop sign, you are on Pleasant Valley Road. You will come to a crossroad with a big, blue, three-storey hotel ahead on the corner. This building is the Armstrong Hotel, built in 1892. You are in the older part of town and if you have the time, stop and wander through the old shops.

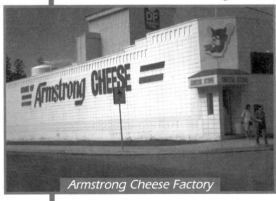
Armstrong Cheese Factory

Turn to your right, cross the railway tracks and then turn to your left. The road curves around the curling rink and you will come to the Armstrong Cheese Factory on the right side of the road. It is a white building with red lettering.

You walk in the door and straight ahead of you are big windows through which you can watch the cheese being made and packaged. You can buy the various types of cheese right from the store. In a back room, set on a table, are some trophies and ribbons the company has won over the years. Beside them are some cheese recipes for you to pick up.

CHEESE FACTS

To make 0.45 kilograms (1 pound) of cheese requires 5 litres (10 pounds) of milk. Cheese has been a food staple for centuries, with the nomadic tribes in Asia being credited with its creation. Although the equipment has become more efficient, the basic process for making cheese has not changed. The steps are processing the milk, separating the curd, ripening and packaging.

Although there are only five groups of cheeses – soft, semi-soft, firm, fresh and hard – over 400 different types are available to Canadian consumers. The more moisture that is removed from the cheese, the harder it becomes. It takes two to three months to age mild cheese, more than a year for aged, and over 18 months for extra aged. For the best flavour, let the cheese warm to room temperature before serving.

If you are in Armstrong on the Thanksgiving long weekend, watch for the brightly coloured reds, blues, yellows, purples and oranges of the hot air balloons riding on the air currents in the sky above you. This is the annual Armstrong Hot Air Balloon Rendezvous, which attracts pilots from BC, Alberta and the northwestern USA. The balloons lift off from the Highland Park School grounds and if you are one of the lucky ones, you might be able to charter a ride in one.

Bobsled Park

O'Keefe Ranch

South of Armstrong you enter the District of Spallumcheen. At kilometre 8.3 (mile 5.1) from Armstrong you come to the turn to Rogers Cereal and Flour Mill. Half-hour tours are offered on Wednesdays at 10 am and on Fridays at 2 pm. It is best to call ahead (phone (604) 546-8744). The tour consists of a video that shows the process of milling the grain from when it arrives until it is packaged, and a visit to a viewing room from which you can watch part of this process live. There is also a bulk food store, which is open 8 am to 5 pm on weekdays and 10 am to 4 pm on weekends.

The mill was started by the Rogers family in the 1950s. In the late 1980s it was sold to Nisshin Flour Milling, which has its head office in Japan.

Three kilometres (1.8 miles) from the Rogers Mill you come to Bobsled Park, the only stainless steel bobsled run in Canada. At the park you are towed up to the top and then rush down part of the 540 metres (1770 feet) of track. There are also go-carts, horseback riding, gold panning, a picnic area and a snack bar.

When you reach the junction with Highway 97, turn west and go 4.2 kilometres (2.6 miles) to the historic O'Keefe Ranch. This ranch was founded in 1867 by Cornelius O'Keefe and Thomas Greenhow. For a century it grew and prospered until it was the largest cattle empire in the Okanagan. It had amassed about 8100 hectares (20,000 acres) at its height. The ranch has since been turned over to the City of Vernon as a historic site.

If you are planning a wedding, St. Anne's Church, built on the ranch in 1889, is available for bookings. You can tour the 12 original buildings, including the log home that the O'Keefes first lived in, a blacksmith shop and the O'Keefe mansion. Stop and visit with the interpreters; they are dressed in period clothing.

OKANAGAN WINE FESTIVAL

In late September-early October the Okanagan Wine Festival is held for 10 days. There are over 40 events including cooking demonstrations, champagne brunches, grapestomps, vineyard picnics, elegant dinners and consumer testing. This event has become so popular that it has been included in the American Bus Association's list of 'top 100 events' in Canada and the USA.

The Okanagan has 22 wineries, which are divided into three categories. Those in the Farmgate category must use 100% BC grown grapes with 75% of them coming from their own vines. They are permitted to produce between 4546 litres and 45,460 litres (1000 and 10,000 gallons) of wine per year.

The Estate wineries also must make their wine from BC grown grapes with 50% coming from their vineyards. They can produce up to 181,840 litres (40,000 gallons) of wine.

Wineries in the Commercial category have few restrictions.

VERNON

Farm Shop and Bakery, Vernon

Continue south on Highway 97. To visit Vernon's Magnetic Hill, as you come into town turn left on 43rd Avenue and follow it to Pleasant Valley Road, which is a four-way stop, and turn left. Follow Pleasant Valley about three blocks until you reach BX Road and turn to your right. This street wanders through residences and orchards and is a great way to see the fruit trees up close. When you pass East Vernon Road, start watching for Briggs Road. Turn left on it and then left again on Dickson Dam Road.

You are now between Hartnell and Hughes roads. Drive 0.3 kilometre (0.2 miles) until you see a row of seven alder trees on your left. You will be facing down a hill. Go to the second last tree and put your vehicle in neutral and you will begin to back up the hill. Try it again, if you don't believe it. And if you still are shaking your head, drive to Hughes Road, turn around, and come back to that same tree. You will be facing uphill. Put it into neutral and watch yourself climb up that hill.

If you are hungry and want to eat something wholesome after munching on junk food all day, return to Highway 97 and continue south for four blocks. Turn left off the highway onto 39th Avenue and drive one block to 30th Street. On the northeast corner, in a cream-coloured, two-storey house with green trim, is the Farm Shop, a bakery and restaurant. The Farm Shop sells all-natural breads made from grains milled on the farm, jams and preserves, meat, meat pies, ice cream, and fresh or frozen meals. All items are additive free and produce is bought from farms that grow natural or organic foods. The cheese buns are good. The Farm Shop is open till 5 pm on weekdays and till 4 pm on Sundays.

The highway follows Kalamalka Lake and then Wood Lake as it heads south. It passes through Oyama, Okanagan Centre and Winfield. At kilometre 13 (mile 8) from Vernon, you leave the North Okanagan Regional District and enter the South Okanagan Regional District, where fruit can ripen up to two weeks earlier.

FRUIT

An estimated 27% of the visitors to the Okanagan Valley come because of the fruit. There are over 2000 tree fruit growers in the Okanagan, Creston and Similkameen Valleys. Fruit from British Columbia is sold in over 30 countries.

Apricots bloom first but cherries are the first to ripen. Picking of cherries begins in late June in the south and in early July in the north. Apricots ripen early-to-late July in the south and in mid-July in the north. Throughout the Okanagan, peaches can be picked beginning in late July, pears are harvested between mid-August and mid-September, and apples ripen in September. Peaches, pears and apples ripen the earliest around Osoyoos.

KELOWNA

Kelowna is the largest and oldest city in the Okanagan. It was established in 1859 by Father Pandosy, who came to start an Oblate Mission. It is believed he planted the first apple trees and vineyards in the Okanagan. He taught the Natives and encouraged settlers to come to the area. The Pandosy Mission has been a heritage site since 1983 and a church and some buildings still remain.

One of the oldest homes in the city was built by the Earl and Countess of Aberdeen. They had visited the area before the Earl was appointed Governor General of Canada in 1883, and in 1891 they bought 480 acres. They built Guisachan House, which was named after Lady Aberdeen's hometown and means 'place of the firs' in Gaelic. However, they never lived in the house. The ranch, as well as the Coldstream Ranch east of Vernon, which they also owned, were managed by her brother. The old house has been refurbished and you can stop in for lunch or dinner.

To reach the Kettle Valley Railway trestles, turn left onto Gordon Road and drive down to KLO Road. ('KLO' stands for Kelowna Land and Orchard Co.) Turn left onto it and follow it to McCulloch Road. Stay on this road past Gallagher Canyon Golf Course to Myra Road and turn right. (See Chapter 7 for more information.)

WESTSIDE ROAD

Westside Ferry landing site

As you leave Kelowna you cross Okanagan Lake on a floating bridge. Stay in the right-hand lane and at the set of lights turn right onto Westside Road. This beautiful drive north along the west side of Okanagan Lake has the road sometimes down at the lakeshore and sometimes high above it. A lot of heritage is being lost, though, as resorts, summer homes and permanent residences are being built over historic sites.

The first turn to your right is the Old Ferry Wharf Road. You drive down to a dead end but there are a couple of old wharves with their huge timbers still out in the water. This site used to be the Westside Ferry Landing.

At Bear Creek Provincial Park the campground is on the right. Across from it is a picnic area and parking for those who want to hike some of the 20 or so kilometres (about 12 miles) of trails through the Bear Creek Canyon.

One and one half kilometres (0.9 miles) from the canyon is Brown's Road. Down on the lakeshore was Wilson Landing, the first of the steamboat landings on the lake. The area is residential now and there is nothing to show that it once was an historic site.

Watch for the road to the Girl Guide Camp 3.8 kilometres (2.4 miles) from Brown's Road. Park on the highway

Bear Creek Canyon

if the gate is closed; as you walk down the driveway, there will be a fence to your right. When you reach the gate in the fence go through it and you will be on a path that was part of the old Brigade Trail. The Brigade Trail was the route the fur traders followed when hauling their furs to the forts. Turn to the right and climb

up the slight hill and you will see a painted sign of a horse and rider tacked to a tree. This part of the trail is now used as a riding path.

Four kilometres (2.5 miles) from the camp is a curve in the road just past a speed limit sign, and there will be a gravel road to your right. You make a sharp turn onto this road, which heads downhill. This road is to Caesars, the second of the sternwheeler landings on the lake. A number of roads crisscross it and there are no

Brigade Trail at Girl Guide camp

Old corral

houses. It looks like the area is used as an informal campsite, but it is kept clean. At the lake are some blackened pilings sticking out of the water, all that is left of the dock.

Nahun, at one time the most populous of the landing towns, is down Deighton's Road, 1.5 kilometres (0.9 miles) from Ceasars Road. The lane is narrow and obviously not built for vehicles. Only one residence is there now.

That beautiful rock wall as you drive north, with its different mauves, peaches, greys and light greens, is part of Mauvais Rocher, a steep rock cliff that blocked the journeys of many settlers coming into the area.

At kilometre 3.9 (mile 2.4) from Deighton Road, look to your left and you will see an old corral in the bush. Many people believe that this is one of the campsites used by David Douglas, the botanist after whom the Douglas-fir is named, when he came through the area in 1833.

There is nothing left to see of Ewing Landing and the rest of the road is through farms, ranches and orchards; it ends at Highway 97.

Back on Highway 97, south of Kelowna, just south of Westside Road, watch for Westlake Road. To see Butterfly World and Parrot Island turn right onto Westlake Road. Take the second right into the parking lot.

At the entrance into Butterfly World is a list of which butterflies will be emerging and the dates. This way you will know what to watch for, or if you want to see a certain species, when to return.

Butterfly World

Butterfly World is very tropical inside, much like a greenhouse. The butterflies fly freely and you can study them closely when they alight on a bench or rock, or drink nectar from the flowers. They also like the fermented fruit at the feeding station.

Parrot Island

The tour is self-guided and there is much to see inside and out. Besides the butterflies there is a pond with several turtles, a beehive, jungle bugs, a waterfall, a gazebo, gardens and a patio where you can buy refreshments. In the gift shop you can buy numerous items shaped like butterflies, books on butterflies and various souvenirs.

Parrot Island is right next to Butterfly World. Inside the gift shop everything is about parrots, including stuffed parrots, books on parrots and T-shirts with parrot pictures.

The exotic birds in this paradise are bred and hand-raised here.

Many of them talk and are very friendly. Some will sit on the back of a bench behind you while others will settle on your arm or let you hold them. They include toucans, lories, macaws and Australian parakeets.

WESTBANK TO PENTICTON

WESTBANK AND PEACHLAND

As you near Westbank, to the left you have a great view of Okanagan Lake with the hills behind. You come into Westbank on a one-way street, so you do not have to contend with oncoming traffic. This town is the only one along this route with the highway divided into one-ways through it. As you leave you come to

Peachland Museum

the meeting of Highway 97C with Highway 97. If you want to go to Merritt, get into the right lane. Keep in the left-hand lane to go to Peachland.

Turn in at the road into Peachland and head down to the lake. Turn right onto Beach Avenue and drive slowly, enjoying the

Okanagan Lake

sandy beach, blue water and hills beyond. Park and get out and walk in the sand or sit on one of the benches and dream of having this view outside your front window. Beach Avenue offers a lovely, long drive beside the shore of Okanagan Lake, through the main part of Peachland.

At the south end of town is the Peachland Museum in the former Baptist Church. This impressive, eight-sided building was constructed in 1910 and now has exhibits of the first orchards in the Okanagan.

Continue past the museum and you will come back onto the highway.

A world-record kokanee was caught in Okanagan Lake in 1986. It weighed 4.3 kilograms (9.4 pounds) and the record is waiting to be broken. Or try for rainbow trout. They weigh up to 13.6 kilograms (30 pounds). For kokanee and rainbow trout, trolling is best. If you want some action, try fishing for Okanagan carp with a light tackle.

Just about everyone has heard of Ogopogo, the creature said to live in Okanagan Lake. Well, if you want to see his home waters, stop in at the viewpoint 2 kilometres (1.2 miles) south of Peachland. You will be looking out over Squally Point. Many people claim to have seem him and some even have pictures to prove he exists. As near as anyone can figure out he is 0.3-0.6 metres (1-2 feet) in diameter and between 4.5 and 15 metres (15 and 50 feet) long. His head is that of a bearded goat or bearded horse. Get your binoculars out and see if you can confirm one of those descriptions.

OGOPOGO

Native peoples believed the fierce lake monster N'ha-a-itk lived in a cave in the deep waters off Squally Point. They would fearfully paddle out to the point and slip small animals over the sides of their canoes in an effort to appease the creature.

According to their legend Ogopogo was a man who, while possessed by a demon, killed another man named Old Kan-He-K at the lake. The angry gods turned the murderer into a giant serpent that would live in the lake. They wanted him to always be where he committed the murder.

The serpent was first seen in the early 1800s. In 1860, a team of horses being swum across the lake was pulled under, never to be seen again. Everyone believed the lake monster got them.

SUMMERLAND

The 560 kilometre (350 mile) Kettle Valley Railway ran from Midway north through Summerland to Princeton and on to Spences Bridge northwest of Merritt. When air travel became popular, the railway slowly began to close the line down. It made its final long distance trip from Midway to Spences Bridge on January 17, 1964. The tracks from Midway to Penticton were torn up a few years after that line closed in 1972.

Kettle Valley Railway car

The line from Okanagan Falls to Penticton and on to Spences Bridge finally shut down in 1989. But in an effort to save some of the grand heritage, the Kettle Valley Railway Heritage Society has restored some old cars, brought in a couple of engines from Duncan, and now offers tours on some of the preserved railway line from Summerland to Faulder.

To reach the station turn right onto Rosedale at the first set of lights past the information centre. Go through the four-way stop and you will be on

Kettle Valley Railway tracks

Prairie Valley Road. At the next four-way stop, turn left and you are on Victoria Road. Follow it to the railway station. If you don't want to take a ride but want to see some of the old track and a trestle, carry on down Victoria to Lewes, which is at a T intersection. Turn right onto Lewes, then left onto Hillborn. Drive to Canyon View Road and turn right. You will pass Summerland Sweets and come to the railway tracks all in about one block.

The original wicket wall from the West Summerland Kettle Valley Railway Station is now in the Summerland Museum on Wharton Street.

Summerland Sweets has 14 different fruit syrups, 15 gourmet jams, jellies, dried fruits, and three flavours of fruit candies. Goodies come in different sizes of jars and you can have gift boxes made up.

That big hill you see in the centre of town is called Giant's Head; it is the core of an extinct volcano. It is possible to drive to the top and have a spectacular view of Peachland to the north, Penticton to the south, Okanagan Lake and Summerland below. To reach the hill from Summerland Sweets, drive back to Hillborn Street, turn

Orchard, Summerland

View from Giant's Head

left and then take the right onto Giant's Head Road. Drive until Milne Road and turn left. This route will take you to the entrance to Giant's Head Park. The gates close at 6 pm so make sure that you have plenty of time to get to the top and back again before the park closes.

The 3.2 kilometre (2 mile) climb up to the top is on one lane of asphalt that hugs the mountain side and has some sheer drop-offs. It was constructed as a Canada Centennial project in 1967. You go through sparse ponderosa pine at the beginning then you move into Douglas-fir further up. At the top is a parking lot.

For those who want to get to the viewpoint quickly from the parking lot, there is a steep path straight up. If you want to take it more slowly and easily, a path crisscrosses its way to the top. Benches are placed along the path so you can relax and enjoy the sights.

At the summit is a fence, a cairn and a superb view of the orchards and lake below. The wind gets pretty strong up there so you might have to sit down to take your pictures. The cairn was built in 1967 and inside is a time capsule to be opened on its 100th anniversary.

Sagebrush along Okanagan Lake

SUMMERLAND TO PRINCETON ROAD

If you want to travel some of the old Kettle Valley Railway route, take the Summerland-to-Princeton road, which parallels the railbed. It leaves the west end of Summerland on Bathfield Road. There is pavement for the first 7.4 kilometres (4.6 miles), then gravel. The road is sometimes narrow. The scenery includes hills, trees and valleys, and you cross many creeks.

At about 21 kilometres (13 miles) is the Trout Creek Recreation Site. You will reach a yield sign at kilometre 37.8 (mile 23.5). To your right is a slight hill. Climb up it and you will be on the old Kettle Valley Railway bed. Turn left at the yield sign and you will go down into Thirsk Lake Recreation Site.

The road follows the bed and you can see the rocky slope of it through the trees. five kilometres (3 miles) from the yield sign the road crosses the old railway bed and then you come to an intersection of gravel roads. You can turn right to go to Peachland if you wish.

The gravel lasts for another 2 kilometres (1.2 miles) and then you reach pavement. The road follows Osprey and Chain lakes for a ways. Eighty-nine kilometres (55 miles) from Summerland you reach Princeton.

PENTICTON

SS Sicamous *in Penticton*

As you come into Penticton you can see the sternwheeler *SS Sicamous* and the barge *Naramata* lined up along the lakeshore. When you cross the bridge, take the first left and follow it to the lake.

The *Sicamous* is 61.1 metres (200.5 feet long), 12.2 metres (40 feet) wide, 2.4 metres (8 feet) deep and weighs 1620 tonnes (1786 tons). It was launched on May 26, 1914. On its voyages the engines burned up about 15 tonnes (17 tons) of coal. It travelled at about 31 kilometres per hour (17 knots or 20 miles per hour) and could carry up to 350 passengers. It had a dining room, four sa-

Beach in Penticton

loons and 36 staterooms. Its last commercial trip was on October 11, 1936. After it was dry-docked at Penticton in 1951, it was used as a cafe, a wax museum and a night club before being restored.

The *Naramata* is 27.4 metres (89.8 feet) long, 5.9 metres (19.5 feet) wide, has a 2.4 metre (8 feet) draft, and weighs 136 tonnes (149.9 tons). It ran a barge transfer service until 1965 and is now open for the public to tour.

Both have steel hulls and were prefabricated in the Port Arthur, Ontario, shipyards and shipped to Okanagan Landing by train to be reassembled in the CPR shipyards.

The boats are right on the lakeshore and there is a lovely beach for you to relax on and soak up some sun. Right beside the boats is the Penticton rose garden. The roses come in pink, red, burgundy, purple, white and every colour in between. Stroll through them; they are just gorgeous.

OKANAGAN WINERIES

The warm climate and long growing season of the Okanagan has led to years of planting and harvesting a wide variety of fruit in the region. But fruit isn't the only product the Okanagan is famous for. Its more than 20 wineries produce a wide variety of wines and many of these are excellent enough to challenge the might of the French wines.

The first grapevines were planted in 1899 by botanist G.W. Henry. Twenty-seven years later, a Kelowna rose grower named J.W. Hughes planted the first vineyard in the Okanagan. This vineyard was on the same site as the first apple orchard set out by Father Charles Pandosy in 1862.

Little was done until Dr. Eugene Rittich, a Hungarian who had worked in the wine industry in France, Austria and Germany, moved to the Okanagan in the early 1930s. His experience helped the wine makers in British Columbia improve their trade.

Eland at Penticton Game Farm

As you drive through Penticton on Highway 97, you will be beside the Channel Parkway. It links Okanagan Lake with Skaha Lake and on hot days people are out on the channel in tubes, rafts, dinghies, canoes, or what have you, floating along between the two lakes. You cross the channel right at Skaha Lake and you can see the beautiful sandy beaches to your left.

Pen-tak-tin meant 'a place to stay' to the Salish people.

Five kilometres (3 miles) south of Penticton is the turn into the Okanagan Game Farm. The farm has 243 hectares (600 acres) of land. You can walk or drive on the 5 kilometres (3 miles) of road through it. There are 120 species of wildlife from Africa, Asia, South America and North America, giving the farm over 1000 animals and birds. Your children will love the petting zoo. Plan for up to three hours to see the whole farm, so make sure you have the time.

OKANAGAN FALLS TO OSOYOOS

OKANAGAN FALLS

Okanagan Rose Garden, Okanagan Falls

The Okanagan Falls themselves disappeared years ago when the flood control dam was put in to control the level of the water that flows south from here. However, the town is still thriving and it turned 100 years old in 1993.

To see the Memorial Rose Garden and Bassett House, just follow the highway until you come to the Legion on the right side. In the yard of the Legion is the rose garden. Across the highway is Bassett House.

Bassett House is the little grey house in the museum yard. It was ordered from the T. Eaton Co. catalogue in 1909 by the Bassett family, which ran a stage-coach and freighting business. It left the

Basset House, Okanagan Falls

East by train, crossed Okanagan Lake on a sternwheeler, and reached the falls by way of horse and wagon.

Most of the way down to Oliver there are orchards and fruit stands on both sides. This is true orchard country.

OLIVER

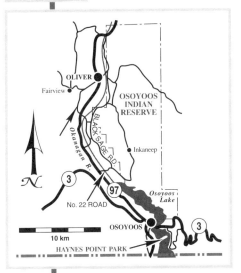

Oliver began as a settlement for veterans of the First World War. In 1921, BC Premier John Oliver set up the South Okanagan Lands Project, which eventually totalled about 8100 hectares (20,000 acres) of irrigated land. The veterans constructed a dam on the Okanagan River north of the community and dug 'the Ditch,' a canal that is still in use today.

As you enter Oliver look ahead and you will see the rock face of McIntyre Bluff or 'Indian Head.' According to Native legend, invading warriors were distracted and almost blinded by lights from the valley. They fell to their death over the 260 metre (850 foot) cliff. Watch for a small herd of California bighorn sheep on the cliffs. They can be recognized by their light brown coats and white rumps.

Desert between Oliver and Osoyoos

In 1890 the Stemwinder claim was staked and a town was established on a bench with a great view of the valley and Osoyoos Lake. It was given the name Fairview. The miners were after lode gold, not placer, and a five-stamp quartz mill was built in 1891–92. The gold rush began with the news that there were three ledges 1 to 2 metres (3 to 6 feet) wide and running parallel to each other for 4.8 kilometres (3 miles).

By 1896, it was realized that the high grade gold was only in isolated areas. In 1902 the Fairview Hotel, called 'the Big Teepee,' burned. The town peaked in 1904 and slowly declined after that. Many businesses moved to Oliver, which was founded in 1921. By 1950 the only one left in the town was John Henry 'Stuttering' Daniels. He had worked his three claims for over 50 years and shared his small cabin with his horse. Finally, he too moved away. The Fairview jail was moved to the museum in Oliver and the town disappeared.

To get to the old Fairview site you go to the set of lights at 350th Avenue and turn right. You will be on Fairview Road. This road takes you past orchards and up into the arid hills above the town. At about 1.6 kilometres (1 mile) you come to the site of the old town, which is marked by a historic sign.

MCKINNEY GOLD

Camp McKinney was linked to Midway to the east by the Meyerhoff stagecoach line and to Fairview to the west by the Halls Line stage. The two roads to these towns met about 3.2 kilometres (2 miles) from Camp McKinney. Gold bullion was regularly shipped from the Cariboo-Amelia Mine stamp mill, which operated around the clock, to San Francisco.

One day in August 1896, George McCauley, one of the mine's shareholders, began the trip to Midway in his buckboard with three gold bars in a gunny sack. Near the meeting of the trails a masked man armed with a rifle jumped out of the trees and demanded the gold. McCauley threw down the bars and continued driving as he had been ordered.

After investigations, a miner named Matt Roderick, who had claimed to be sick on the day of the robbery, fell under suspicion. Roderick, a quiet man who always lost his pay cheque to gambling, left town a couple of days later with just his bedroll and owing a friend for his ticket back to his home in Tacoma, Washington. However, once home he paid off taxes owing against his house and began gambling. Pinkertons, hired by the mine, believed that he had smuggled out one gold bar in his bedroll and would soon return to Camp McKinney for the others.

In October, word spread that Roderick was on his way to the camp from Fairview. Two men from the mine headed out on the Fairview Road to meet him and take him in for questioning. They caught up with a man heading west towards Fairview and leading a horse. When accosted, he didn't answer.

There was a shot and the man, who turned out to indeed be Matt Roderick, fell dead. One of the men, mine superintendent Joseph Keane, claimed he had had to shoot or Roderick would have shot him. It was found that Roderick's rifle had grease rags plugging it and his six shooter was rusty, so he would not have been able to shoot Keane. Furthermore, no gold bars were found on him.

There are many unanswered questions about the affair. If Roderick was the highwayman, why was he leaving the area with just his guns and his saddlebags empty? Had he only come just to retrieve his guns or was he on his way to where he had stashed the gold when shot? Why did the superintendent shoot so quickly? Was he an accomplice?

Whatever the answers to these questions, the gold bars could still be hidden somewhere along the McKinney Road.

Haynes Ranch

Another old gold town, founded in 1887 high up near the summit of Mount Baldy, is Camp McKinney. To reach the camp road turn left on 350th Avenue. You cross a bridge and see an H sign for Hospital. Turn right and follow the road past the hospital. Watch for the sign that says Black Sage Road. Cross Black Sage Road and you are on Camp McKinney Road.

Back in Oliver, continue south on Highway 97 and you will be surrounded by orchards. There is the occasional fruit stand but most of these orchards have a driveway right up to the house.

The Sonoran Desert runs north from Mexico, through the United States and into Canada. The southern Okanagan is part of the Upper Sonoran Desert Zone which, in Canada, is known as the Arid Biotic area. Around Oliver the animals closely resemble those on the mountain plateaus of Mexico. The burrowing owl, five-toed kangaroo rat, Lord pocket mouse, black-nosed bat, horned toad and Townsend jack-rabbit are not found anywhere else in Canada.

The Osoyoos area gets little more than 20 cm (8 inches) of precipitation each year so the plants growing here, like the animals, are not found elsewhere in the country. The most easily identifiable are the sagebrush and greasewood (also called black sagebrush or bitterbrush). An obvious difference is that sagebrush blooms in the fall while the greasewood blooms in the spring. Cacti bloom in late June and that is when you can see just how many plants there are in the sagebrush flats. The blossoms are large, waxy, and mainly yellow, with some having pink tints.

The highly successful orchards are a result of irrigation.

At kilometre 9.5 (mile 5.9) from Oliver you come to No. 22 Road. Turn left onto it. Watch for groups of birdwatchers. Their vehicles will be parked along the road and they will be wandering with their cameras and binoculars looking for bobolink, meadowlark, snipe, lazuli buntings, canyon wrens, Canada's smallest hum-

Black Sage Road

mingbird, and Bullock's orioles in the meadows. These meadows are where the brigades of fur traders used to camp overnight before crossing the channelled Okanagan River in the morning.

You will cross a one-lane, wooden bridge and 1.6 kilometres (1 mile) from the highway you reach a T intersection and the Black Sage Road. Those two old buildings on the right are all that is left of Haynes Ranch, which was established here in 1882. When fire destroyed the first house, wood had to be brought by barge across two lakes and by river from the Okanagan Mission to replace it.

If you turn left and follow the Black Sage Road, it will take you back through the desert to Oliver. If you turn right, the road leads to the Osoyoos Indian Reserve. On the reserve is the Pocket Desert, a piece of the desert that has been kept in its natural state. You should ask permission of the band before venturing too far onto the reserve.

Along the Black Sage Road you will see the desert on your left and on the right, at times, lush grass watered by Osoyoos Lake. If you decide to do any walking around the desert make sure you wear high-top boots because this is rattlesnake and scorpion country.

DESERT SURVIVAL

In the desert, plants do not grow close together. The absence of water is partly the cause, but there is another reason. The plants themselves prevent overcrowding. When the seeds of some annual plants come in contact with water, the seed jackets emit a chemical that enables the seed to germinate, but hinders the seeds of other plants from getting started.

The roots of the greasewood inject a substance into the soil around it that is poisonous to other plants. The ponderosa pine sucks up the moisture from the soil, stopping even its own seedlings from growing nearby. The most dominant plant, the sagebrush, discharges a growth inhibitor into the air around it which prevents seeds from growing too close.

OSOYOOS

Osoyoos is at the southern end of the Okanagan. The fruit produced in this area is the first in Canada to ripen.

On the east end of town along Highway 3 towards Grand Forks, there is a tall windmill. Here in a separate building is A Touch of Holland Bakery and Gift Shop. The smell as you walk in is heavenly. The bakery has danishes, cakes, squares, all types of breads, buns, pies, tarts, everything you can imagine.

Touch of Holland Bakery, Osoyoos

The windmill, surrounded by lawn and flowers, is a replica of a Dutch windmill built in 1816. Tours of it are available so ask at the bakery. To the west is a picnic area along the shore of Osoyoos Lake where you can enjoy your fresh-bought goods.

If you want to camp for the night, go south on Highway 97, past the junction with Highway 3, to 32nd Avenue. Turn left and in a few blocks you will be driving on a causeway out into Osoyoos Lake, towards fully serviced Haynes Point Provincial Park.

CHAPTER 10
OSOYOOS TO KAMLOOPS

Nicola Lake

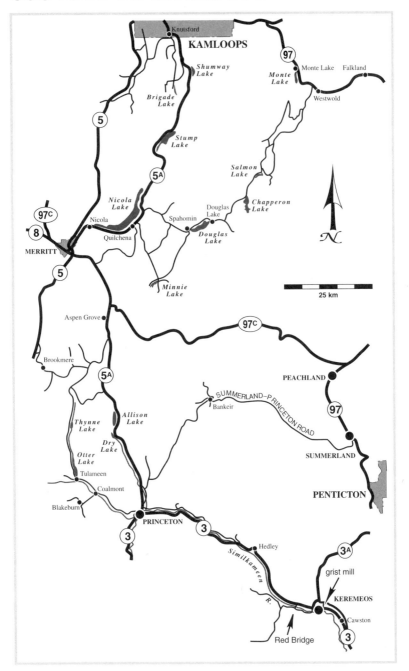

> **This route has an unusual and diverse history. Mining, railways, ranches, camels and tales of bank robbery and murder are all represented. Most of the route will be on gravel roads, with some back country driving. Be prepared for variety.**

OSOYOOS TO PRINCETON

CAWSTON

Just west of Osoyoos on Highway 3 is Cawston. It was originally a Hudson's Bay Company post. Horses were kept here because of the mild winters and abundance of grass. Before the First World War, cattle ranching and fruit growing began and a cannery was built to process tomatoes. Tobacco and mangels, a beet-type vegetable used for cattle feed, were tried but failed owing to the Depression. There are many orchards and fruit stands between this town and Keremeos.

KEREMEOS

Keremeos, on the banks of the Similkameen River, is known as 'the Fruit Stand Capital of Canada.' There are orchards with fruit stands, and orchards where you can pick your own fruit.

To get to the Grist Mill, turn onto Highway 3A when you reach the junction. Follow the road and the signs to the parking lot. This mill was built in 1877 by Barrington Price. It has been restored with the water wheel and flume being reconstructed. Look inside the upper floor and see the belts and pulleys that were turned by

water flowing from the flume over the water wheel. These belts and pulleys worked the vertical stone grinder, which ground the wheat into flour. You can buy flour ground by the mill in the store or eat baked goods, made from the flour, in the Tea Room.

Using the tour map obtained at the entrance, take a walk through the apple orchard, which has rare varieties of apples. The wheat fields planted with seeds saved from the previous year so they

Grist Mill

Red Bridge over Similkameen River at Keremeos

are the same variety as our grandparents planted. The exhibit building, also built in 1877, was once the general store of the area. In the display room are different types of grain, cereal boxes on the wall and equipment.

NAMES

This town is the fifth one to have the name Keremeos. The first was founded by the Hudson's Bay Company in the mid-1860s and called Fort Keremeos. In 1872 part of the post was sold to a Mr. Barrington Price and a Mr. Henry Nicholson. They used the post as a ranch and constructed the region's first and only grist mill, which has survived although the post has disappeared.

Also in 1872, Lower Keremeos was founded just west of present-day Highway 3A. It remained there until 1899 when the townspeople moved it between Shuttleworth and Keremeos creeks. Because it was on higher elevation it was named Upper Keremeos. Also in this year Keremeos Centre was founded 3.2 kilometres (2 miles) north of the present town.

When the railway came through, both Upper Keremeos and Keremeos Centre both moved beside the tracks and by 1906 Upper Keremeos had disappeared and the new town was named Lower Keremeos. Eventually the Lower was dropped and it became just Keremeos.

Just west of Keremeos is the turn-off to the historic red bridge. This bridge was built in 1907 by the Great Northern Railway under the name Vancouver, Victoria and Eastern Railway and is western Canada's last covered bridge. It has a wooden deck, is one lane wide, and is now used as a vehicle bridge across the Similkameen River. The banks at the bridge are a good place to go swimming in the river or to launch a tube.

As you continue west on Highway 3, watch for the giant rock, called 'Lovestone' or 'Standing Rock,' on the right side of the highway. It has graffiti all over it and across the road from it is the Standing Rock Native Crafts store in a log building.

Fourteen kilometres (8.7 miles) from Keremeos is the Hubcap Place, which has over 16,000 hubcaps to sell or trade. If you need some, stop in and look around. If you have some to spare, see what kind of a deal you can make.

FIRST NON-NATIVES

Although the credit of being the first non-Native to see the Keremeos Valley is given to Alexander Ross of the Hudson's Bay Company (who nearly died while passing through in 1813), legend has it that the first non-Natives were actually Spaniards.

In the 1700s, a group of Spaniards was shipwrecked at the mouth of the Columbia River, at what is now Astoria, Oregon. The survivors began a northeast trek overland dressed in full armour. When they met up with a band of Native people, they defeated them in a minor battle and continued on their journey. With the coming of the snows, they built a camp near Kamloops. Many died during the winter, owing to illness and further fighting.

In the spring, the remaining Spaniards decided to head back to the coast the same way they had come. In the Keremeos Valley, they met the Native people again. The Natives sought revenge, and this time they won. At the end of the fight, the Native people buried the Spaniards complete with their armour and weapons.

Somewhere in the Keremeos Valley is the yet unfound, and valuable, 'Spanish Mound.'

Old mine site above Hedley

Gold was discovered on Nickel Plate Mountain in 1898 and the town of Hedley was born. In 1904 a stamp mill was built above the town to process the ore from the Nickel Plate Mine, one of the richest gold producers in the province. The Mascot Mine, situated on less than 0.4 hectare (1 acre), also had high yields. The ore body of gold, silver and copper lasted until 1955, when it finally ran out. If you look up on the mountain side to the north you will see some old, abandoned buildings from the Mascot Mine and the cable from the tramway used to haul ore cars down to the town.

If you want to drive a historic route, take the Old Hedley Road to Princeton. It begins 5.8 kilometres (3.6 miles) west of Hedley and can be seen across the Similkameen River from Highway 3 for some of the way.

PRINCETON

For centuries the Okanagan and Nicola First Nations mined the red ochre from this area at the fork of the Similkameen and Tulameen rivers. They used it for their paintings and traded it with other bands. It is not known for sure whether the early fur traders, who used the area as a stopover on their way along the Hudson's

Berm of rock at Copper Mountain Mine

Bay Brigade Trail, or the miners of 1858 who named this place Vermilion Forks. It doesn't matter, though, because the name was changed in 1860 by Governor James Douglas in honour of the expected visit of the Prince of Wales.

PONY EXPRESS

In 1987, communities with the same desires and ambitions on both sides of the border decided to pair up and work together towards common goals. Princeton's 'sister city' is Tonasket, Washington. Because they both have rodeos, they decided to promote those rodeos by having an annual Pony Express Friendship Ride between the two towns.

Five Canadian and five American riders are chosen to participate in the 160 kilometre (100 mile) run and 200 specially designed envelopes, 100 for Canadians and 100 for Americans, are sold. These envelopes, with letters inside them, are placed in an authentic US Postal Service Pony Express bag and stamped at each post office along the route.

The Pony Express ride is in service each year only at rodeo time.

Stagecoach at Princeton Museum

Watch for Copper Mountain Road as you enter Princeton and turn left on it. When you come to a Y intersection, take either fork as they both meet in about 1 kilometre (0.6 mile). The road is paved and at kilometre 5.6 (mile 3.5) you come to the Allenby Road. The early mining company built a concentrating plant at Allenby but there is nothing left to see any more.

In 20 kilometres (12.4 miles) you come to a sharp hairpin turn and you go up a hill to the Similco Mine. Here are some buildings and huge rock berms of grey, black, tan, orangish and copper-coloured rock. There is no sign of the old town of Copper Mountain.

Copper was discovered here in the 1880s, but it wasn't until 1896 that exploration began. Mining companies soon opened. Some did well, others did not. Ore prices fluctuated and the First World War stopped production. Mining was revived in 1923 and in 1952 open-pit mining began. However, low prices forced the closure in 1957 and the mining towns of Copper Mountain and Allenby disappeared. The present mining began in 1979 but no town was built.

Castle Campground entrance

In 1904 the Welby stagecoach line from Hedley to Penticton began. Another coach line, operated by Fred Revely, ran from Hedley to Princeton. One of the original coaches from that era is in the Livery Stables building at the Princeton Museum on Vermilion Avenue. It is now used for parades and special occasions.

To see the Princeton Castle, take Highway 5A north out of town and turn east on to the Summerland Road. Watch for the sign to the Castle RV Park. Turn onto the access road and drive to the park.

THE GENTLEMAN BANDIT

In 1904, a man named George Edwards moved in with Jack Budd on his ranch near Princeton. Edwards was soft spoken, kind, generous, charming, and liked by the people of the town. He enjoyed dancing and playing the fiddle. He tried prospecting and farming but never made a go at either. In spite of this, he always had money.

It was during his long stay at the Budd Ranch that this gentleman planned a train robbery at Ducks, later named Monte Creek, near Kamloops. With the two members of his gang, he headed north and robbed a CPR train on May 8, 1906.

The gang started south and stopped near Douglas Lake for the night. They were tracked by Constable William Fernie and a mounted police posse. When the posse came up to them, 'Edwards' calmly told them they were prospectors from Grand Prairie (now Westwold). But one of his friends cracked under the pressure and ran, firing his revolver in all directions.

They were arrested and after their trial they were sent to the prison in New Westminster. 'Edwards' escaped and fled to the USA where he was captured. After one more escape and recapture 'the Gentleman Bandit,' whose real name was Bill Miner, spent the rest of his life in the prison, dying at Milledgeville, Georgia, on September 2, 1913.

An American bandit, Miner has the distinction of pulling Canada's first train robbery. Before the holdup at Ducks, he and two companions robbed the CPR Transcontinental at Mission, BC on May 10, 1904, making off with $57,000 worth of gold, bonds and money.

There is an exhibit on Bill Miner in the Princeton Museum.

The Portland Cement Plant was built between 1904 and 1908. It cost a million dollars, took thousands of man-hours to construct, and was in operation for only nine months before it closed down. As the building slowly deteriorated, the walls took on the shape of a castle. You can either stay the night at the park and spend time looking at it or you can pay a fee to see it.

The American bandit Bill Miner used the nearby hillside as a hideout.

COALMONT TO ASPEN GROVE

COALMONT

Coalmont Hotel

To follow part of the historic stagecoach route from Princeton to Nicola, go to the end of Bridge Street in Princeton, cross the wooden bridge and turn left on to Tulameen Avenue. This road will take you west to Coalmont, Granite City and Tulameen.

This route was used by Native people, then fur traders and gold prospectors. It opened up when coal was discovered and died when the coal was mined out. The road is old pavement that is not always in the best shape and it is your typical high mountain, back country road.

At kilometre 17.2 (mile 10.7) from Princeton you come to Coalmont, a town built at the turn of the century when the Columbia Coal and Coke Company began mining coal in the area. The railway that laid the track in to haul the coal out was called the Vancouver, Victoria and Eastern, a subsidiary of the Great Northern from the United States.

Coalmont Hotel, built in 1911, is still standing on Main Street.

COAL MINER

Although the presence of coal in the area had been known for years, it was a small animal, resembling a groundhog and called a 'mountain beaver,' that finally was the reason that Coalmont was founded. These animals like to burrow, pushing the dirt and anything else out around the hole.

In 1906, a Welshman named Henry Lowe noticed fragments of coal in the mound at one hole and began to investigate. Three years later the main seam was found at an elevation of 1100 metres (3600 feet).

BLAKEBURN AND GRANITE CITY

Old building at Granite City

To get to Blakeburn and Granite City, you turn right onto Parrish Avenue at the four-way stop in Coalmont. When you reach the end, turn left and then turn right when this road ends. You cross a green and yellow bridge with a wooden deck and then turn left again on Blakeburn Road. Here, the pavement ends.

At kilometre 0.8 (mile 0.5) from the bridge you come to a three-way split in the road. You will recognize this place by the sign that says 'Brigade Trail.' The left road (straight ahead) is called Rice Road. The one to the right of that (the middle one) goes to Granite City. The sharp right road goes to Blakeburn and is part of the Brigade Trail.

The Granite City road is just a short trail with grass growing up between the ruts. It leads to the old town site, where you can still see some of the original log buildings. The town began when a prospector found a gold nugget in Granite Creek in 1885. In its heyday Granite City was the third largest town in BC, with 13 hotels, nine grocery stores, two blacksmiths, a drug store, two jewellers and a population of 2000. According to government reports, $90,000 in placer gold (in late-19th century dollars) was taken out in one four-month stretch.

The boom lasted only three years, with flour gold depleted and the mother-lode never found. By the beginning of the 1900s there were only 30 residents, one hotel and two stores. Most of the town burned in a 1907 fire and the last store was moved to Coalmont in 1912. All that is left now are some decaying old buildings.

Bill Miner and his friends liked to stop in Granite City when they were in the area.

Blakeburn – first called Upper Coalmont – was the town at the mine site while Coalmont was about 500 metres (1600 feet) lower on the mountain. Coal was trammed down to Coalmont and sent out by rail. The Blakeburn mine continued to be heavily worked until an explosion at the No. 4 mine killed 45 men on August 13, 1930. Referred to as 'Black Wednesday,' the day marked the end of the era. Although the mine reopened and produced for several years, the community never recovered. The mine finally shut down in 1940 and Blakeburn closed up, too. In the 1950s an open-pit mine destroyed what was left of the town.

Yvonne de Carlo, Lily Munster in the original 'Munsters' television series, came from Blakeburn.

WHITE IRON

During the search for the flour gold in Granite Creek, a lighter coloured, but similarly heavy mineral was also found in the bottom of the pans. This 'white gold' or 'white iron' was difficult to separate from the real gold, and was cursed by the miners and thrown back in the water with the sand.

Legend has it that one man, a Swede named Johansson, saved his 'white gold' by dropping it in a bucket that he kept beside him. When he left the area he buried the bucket, which was almost full, beside his cabin.

Little did the miners realize that they had found platinum, and that the Tulameen River system and the Amur River in Russia are the only rivers in the world where gold and free platinum are found together. Because of the current industrial demand for platinum, Johansson's bucket, buried somewhere in the Granite City area and containing about 10 kilograms (22 pounds) of platinum, could be worth hundreds of thousands of dollars– if the story is true.

TULAMEEN

From Coalmont, continue northwest to Tulameen. It was first called Campement des Femmes by the Hudson's Bay Company fur traders because it was where the Native women waited for the men to return from trapping and hunting.

Gold was discovered in the area in 1853 but little was done until 1859. In 1860 Governor Douglas offered nine miners a grubstake (food and equipment) to explore the Similkameen Valley looking for gold. He also offered a bonus of £14 sterling to any man who found gold. The men found their gold on the Similkameen's South Fork. By the next year both branches of the Similkameen and some of the Tulameen River had been staked. During the rush, 2000 miners camped at the junction of Otter Creek and Tulameen River which was later known as Otter Flats. In 1901 the community was named Tulameen.

Otter Lake

As you drive through town, you will come to a Y intersection. For a swim in the lake or a picnic, carry on straight and 5 kilometres (3.1 miles) north of town you will reach Otter Lake Provincial Park picnic area. To continue along the stagecoach route and to go to Brookmere, go left at the Y intersection instead.

ICE

Otter Lake freezes solid every winter. In the early 1900s, ice blocks cut from it were used by the Great Northern Railway in its refrigerator cars and shipped to ice houses in Spokane, Washington. However, artificial ice production made the ice chopping obsolete and the last load of ice was hauled on January 20, 1925.

At kilometre 8.4 (mile 5.2) from Tulameen, the pavement changes to gravel. All along this road are old buildings. Some are still being used as sheds while others are just remnants of what they used to be.

About 6 kilometres (3.7 miles) from the beginning of the gravel is the Thynne Lake Ranch. The three-storey home there was once a stopping house on the stagecoach trip from Nicola to Princeton. The passengers left Nicola at 6 am and arrived at Jack Thynne's ranch at 7 pm. Early the next morning they were on their way again, arriving at Granite City at 10 am and Princeton at noon.

BROOKMERE

Watch for the Brookmere Road at kilometre 37.1 (mile 23.1) from Tulameen. The sign is set on the stop sign for the Brookmere traffic but it faces in the opposite direction. Brookmere Road comes out to a T intersection with two signs facing it pointing in each direction. Turn left onto this very narrow, winding, climbing road to do some back country driving to Brookmere. (If you decide not to go to Brookmere, it is 11.9 km (7.4 miles) from the Brookmere turn-off to Highway 5A, which runs from Princeton to Aspen Grove – see sidebar.)

At kilometre 3.5 (mile 2.2) watch out for a large tree on the left. It is right beside the road, and if you get too close you could scrape your vehicle. At kilometre 5.5 (mile 3.4) you will reach a Y intersection. Take the left fork. At kilometre 15.3 (mile 9.5) you cross a cattleguard, the old railway bed and another cattleguard, and then reach a crossroads. Ahead is the Thynne Valley Road, which is used by skidooers. Turn right

Caboose at Brookmere

onto the Coldwater Road and follow the railway bed for about 0.5 kilometres (0.3 miles) into Brookmere.

Brookmere was the divisional point for two railways – the Kettle Valley Railway from Merritt and the Vancouver, Victoria, and Eastern from Princeton. The town had two of everything to accommodate the opposing railways. There were two turntables, two roundhouses, two stations, etc. The only apparatus they shared was the water tower. However, it had two spouts: the south one was for the VV&E and the north one for the KVR.

Brookmere water tower

The names of the streets of the hamlet show that it was once a railway town: Engineer Avenue, Roadhouse Drive, and Conductor Wye, for instance. Brookmere Station, now a private home, still has the Brookmere sign above the doorway. The water tower is still standing and there is a CPR caboose near it. Brookmere has no services.

To get to the Coquihalla Highway (Highway 5), just stay on the same road and drive out the other end of town past the Brookmere Station Road. There is about 6 kilometres (3.7 miles) of gravel, then you are on pavement. Take the Coquihalla north to Merritt, and then follow the signs for Highway 5A northward to reach Nicola and Quilchena.

HIGHWAY 5A FROM PRINCETON

The other route from Princeton, along Highway 5A, is in good condition and the scenery is great. There are many small lakes: McCaffrey Lake, Dry Lake (which has a campground), Borgeson Lake and Allison Lake (within a provincial park). There are ranches, summer residences, permanent homes, hills, valleys, farms and lots of scenery. This road used to be called Highway 5, until the Coquihalla was built in the mid 1980s and took its number.

Aspen Grove is 62 kilometres (38.5 miles) from Princeton. Stay on Highway 97C to Merritt and follow the signs for 5A to Nicola and Quilchena.

NICOLA TO KNUTSFORD

NICOLA AND QUILCHENA

When the CPR decided to build a line up the Nicola Valley in 1894, the value of real estate in the village of Nicola increased. And further up the valley the Quilchena Hotel was built along what was supposed to be the railway route to Kamloops. However, the tracks were built through Forksdale, later renamed Merritt, with only a siding to Nicola.

Nicola has quaint two- and three-storey homes. Watch for St. Andrew's United Church, built in 1876, on the right side of the road. This church is also known (since 1917) as 'the Murray,' in honour of the Reverend George Murray, who had worked tirelessly for this parish. Walk through the small graveyard beside it and see some old gravestones.

Grave at St. Andrew's United Church

As you head north on Highway 5A, you are travelling through the Nicola Valley. It has green fields where it is irrigated and drier hills with sagebrush on them where it is not irrigated. Nicola Lake is one of the deepest in the province and is popular with windsurfers as well as anglers trying for kokanee and trout.

Quilchena Hotel

The Quilchena Hotel is about 20 kilometres (12 miles) north of Nicola. It retains its old charm, complete with the original bar, ladies' parlour and bedrooms and it is open for business. Also here are the Nicola Valley Golf Course, a campsite and a store in an old stone building.

DOUGLAS LAKE

One kilometre (0.6 miles) from the Quilchena Hotel is the Pennask Road, on the right. If you want some back country driving with beautiful, rolling hills, take this road to Douglas Lake. It is all gravel and rough and shouldn't be travelled during a rain storm. (If paved roads are more to your taste, continue north on Highway 5A for an additional 2 kilometres (1.2 miles) and turn right onto the second, shorter road to Douglas Lake.)

John Douglas was a Scotsman who worked as a miner until the 1870s when he began homesteading the area. A later owner named J.B. Greaves was the one who built the ranch into a cattle empire. Over the years, owners of the ranch have acquired over 400,000 hectares (1,000,000 acres) of grassland.

Douglas Lake Ranch

Church in Spahomin

You begin to climb above Nicola Lake and soon are surrounded by rolling hills. Expect to see yellow and purple flowers of various species, sagebrush, clumps of ponderosa pine or Douglas-fir and, depending on the time of year, green or golden grass. Look out for cattle on the road.

At kilometre 19.4 (mile 12.1) from the highway, you will reach a sign that says 'Minnie Lake Ranch, A Division of Douglas Lake Ranch.' Douglas Lake is to the left. Up here you are travelling through commonage reserve, land that was set aside as pasture for cattle owned by both Natives and non-Natives.

At kilometre 34 (mile 21.1), after travelling through this beautiful land, you will see the Native village of Spahomin below. On the left side of town stands the tall steeple of the St. Nicholas Church, built in 1889.

It was near this village that the three McLean brothers and a friend sought refuge in a cabin after killing Constable John Ussher near Kamloops. After days without water or food, surrounded by their pursuers, they gave up and were subsequently hanged at New Westminster for their deed.

Eleven kilometres (6.8 miles) from Spahomin is the village of Douglas Lake. There are homes, a school, some workshops and a general store that was built in the early 1900s and is still in operation. Turn right at the arch and straight down the driveway is the store.

From here you can turn around and drive back to Highway 5A or continue through the rolling country to Westwold.

WESTWOLD AND FALKLAND

The pavement on the road from the village of Douglas Lake to Westwold lasts for another 7.6 kilometres (4.7 miles). At kilometre 14.6 (mile 9.1) you reach Chapperon Ranch, also part of the Douglas Lake Ranch. It was around here that Bill Miner was captured with his two partners.

At kilometre 21 (mile 13) from the village of Douglas Lake you come to Salmon Lake and Salmon Lake Resort, which has campsite, cabins, boat rentals and store. You will be driving beside the Salmon River as it snakes along.

You begin driving down into the Salmon River Canyon at kilometre 29.4 (mile 18.3) and in about 2 kilometres (1.2 miles) you are on the canyon floor. There is rock wall on the left and the river and a rock wall on right. You drive through tall trees and cross the river three times. It is dim and the only way to look is up: up at the tree tops, up at the canyon walls, up at the bit of sky overhead.

At kilometre 38.5 (mile 23.9) you start to climb out of the canyon. At kilometre 46.6 (mile 29) is pavement again and a few kilometres from there you reach Highway 97 near Westwold. It was in the valley near here in 1905 that the last Cariboo camel died.

CARIBOO CAMELS

In 1862, 25 camels were purchased from a San Francisco merchant who had gone to China to buy them in 1860. They were taken to Victoria and then transported across to the mainland. They had been bought as pack animals for Cariboo packers: camels could carry more weight than a horse or mule, and they live on anything. Some did get used for a short time as carriers, but their biggest drawback was that they scared the horses of other packers, causing hardships for their owners.

What exactly happened to all of the camels is unknown. Some escaped and were occasionally seen out in the wilderness. One was mistaken for a grizzly and shot. Some were caught in a blizzard and froze and were buried in a mass grave. One was used at Fort Steele for a couple of years.

Three were turned out to pasture in the Westwold area. Two of these were eventually traded for some horses and the other one died there of old age in 1905.

East of Westwold on Highway 97 is Falkland. As you near the town, look on the mountainside to your left and you will see a big cleared area with a Canadian flag in the centre. The closer you get, the bigger the flag looks. It is the largest free-standing flag in Canada and it was put there by the people of Falkland.

The flag is 8.5 metres (28 feet) high and 17 metres (56 feet) wide. It is made of metal with baked-on enamel colours, with a lumber frame of two-by-sixes. It is set on eight 13.7 metre (45 foot) telephone poles that are held in place by cables to 18 cement blocks, each of which weighs about 2000 kilograms (4500 pounds). All the materials, labour and equipment were donated to build this one-of-a-kind flag 150 metres (500 feet) above the valley floor.

HIGHWAY 5A NORTH OF QUILCHENA

Resuming from where the gravel road to Douglas Lake leaves Highway 5A, you continue up the Nicola Valley beside Nicola Lake, which has picnic areas, campsites and boat launches along it. North of the lake you follow the valley through the semi-arid hillsides with their beautiful grasses and flowers. There are many small lakes along this drive.

At kilometre 11.5 (mile 7.1) from where you resumed up Highway 5A you reach a small pond with a viewing station from which you can look out at the different types of wildlife on the water.

In the 1870s, the grass on these hills, called bunch grass, grew as high as a horse's belly. Some enterprising miners realized that the area would make great ranchland so they bought some cattle and began ranching. The area is still called 'cow country.'

Shumway Lake (see the following story about the McLean brothers) is at kilometre 47 (mile 29.2) from the gravel turn-off for Douglas Lake. And at kilometre 52.9 (mile 34.1) is Jackson Road to the left. You have to watch for it because the sign is small. You can recognize it by the metal building and corrals at the road. Turn onto it.

The road is narrow and goes past some corrals and a hay shed. It is fenced on both sides with horses and cows in the pasture. The road winds through trees, up into the hills, and by a valley.

At kilometre 8.1 (mile 5) you reach Manning Road. Turn left and drive for 0.6 kilometre (0.3 mile). On your left will be a corral and at the end will be a barbed-wire fenced area. At the end of that area is a wood slat gate. Park at that gate and climb through the fence. You will be in a cow pasture so watch where you step.

From the parking lot you can see a power line in the distance to your right. Follow the old ruts in a southeasterly direction towards those power lines. You will come to another fence with a gate. Climb through this fence and walk straight towards the power pole in front of you. Continue walking past the pole and around the clump of trees on the left. Behind those trees is the monument that marks the spot where Constable John Ussher met his death.

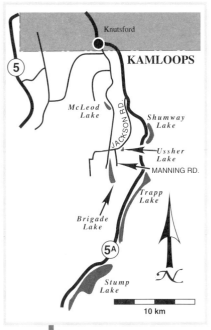

In December 1879 the McLean brothers – Charlie, 17, Archie, 15 and Allan, 25 – and a friend, Alex Hare, 17, stole a horse southeast of Kamloops. When the owner of the horse, William Palmer, spotted them, he rode to town to report the theft to Constable Ussher of the BC Provincial Police. Ussher made Palmer and a tracker named Shumway special constables. Shumway, a man who refused to carry a gun, picked up their trail and followed it until dark. The posse passed by John McLeod's camp near dusk and he joined them. Around noon the next day the four men came upon the gang hiding in the trees. The McLeans and Hare began firing, missing Palmer but hitting McLeod in the cheek and knee, and shooting his horse. Palmer returned the fire.

Ussher cairn

Stump Lake

Constable Ussher's horse reared, leaving him on the ground without a rifle. He walked towards the gang empty handed and asked them to surrender. He tried to grab Hare, who stabbed him repeatedly. Archie McLean ran from behind a tree and shot Ussher in the head. Palmer, the injured McLeod, and pacifist Shumway decided to ride back to Kamloops for help. The murderers took Ussher's clothes, horse and gun, then rode away. They stopped in at a few homesteads in the area and bragged about their feat before taking aim and shooting an old shepherd named James Kelly, near Stump Lake.

The gang then headed to Douglas Lake, where they holed up in a cabin near Spahomin. Meanwhile, another posse had been organized in Kamloops. Led by Justice of the Peace John Clapperton, they headed for Douglas Lake. After a few days without water and food, the gang surrendered. They were tried and hanged in New Westminster.

One kilometre (0.6 mile) from Manning Road you reach a T intersection. To the left the road goes to Brigade Lake and to the right it heads towards Kamloops and Highway 5A.

BRIGADE TRAIL

During the fur trade, men of the Hudson's Bay Company travelled along the Brigade Trail taking their furs to a fort where they could be shipped east. Sometimes as many as 20 men on horseback led 300 packhorses. These packhorses carried several bales of furs weighing 40 kilograms (88 pounds) each. The brigade was commanded by the chief trader and was prodded along by a bagpiper.

At the end of each day's travel they reached their designated campsites where the grass was good for their horses and there was plenty of water and room to spread out. Brigade or Long Lake was the first stop from Kamloops along this trail.

CHAPTER 11
KAMLOOPS TO GOLDEN

Enchanted Forest

KAMLOOPS TO GOLDEN

There are many ways to enter southern Interior British Columbia. Kamloops is at the north end of the Coquihalla Highway. The land is semi-arid, the vegetation is sparse, and the hills look like badlands. But near Chase, trees dominate the landscape. You will see waterfalls, hike trails and climb mountains before reaching the end of this trip.

KAMLOOPS TO SALMON ARM

MONTE CREEK, PRITCHARD AND CHASE

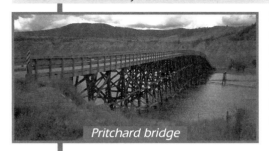
Pritchard bridge

Head east on Highway 1 out of Kamloops. You soon reach Monte Creek, which used to be called Ducks. It is where Bill Miner, Canada's first train robber, held up a CPR train in 1906. (See Chapter 11 for details.)

When you reach the flashing amber light at Pritchard, turn left (north) and you will come to a wooden trestle bridge. The bridge is arched and has a concrete deck. It is one lane and you cannot see if anyone is coming from the other side. At the top, however, the bridge widens and the traffic up there has to yield to the traffic coming up. You pull over into the wider area and wait for the vehicles to pass before continuing down. There is a wooden sidewalk for pedestrians.

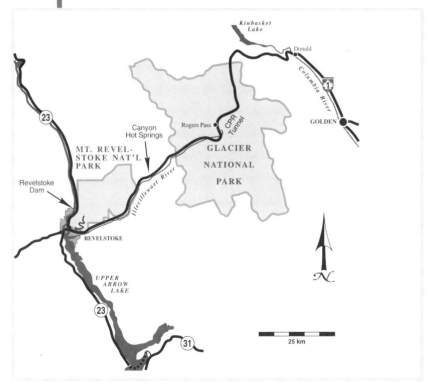

On the other side of the river is a road that goes from Kamloops to Chase, a back country alternative to Highway 1.

Chase is called 'the Gateway to the Shuswap.' At the west end of town are sandy beaches, a boat

Chase Creek Falls

launch and a public pier. Past the first entrance into town, which is on the north side of the highway, stop in at the Chase Creek Rest Area, on the right side of the highway. There are picnic tables and you can walk a short distance beside the creek to see the Chase Falls.

Heading east on Highway 1, you will notice that the vegetation is getting greener and lusher. At kilometre 9.1 (mile 5.7) from Chase take the turn-off to Adams Lake and to Shuswap Lake and Roderick Haig-Brown provincial parks. Then watch for the left turn to Adams Lake.

Mining relics

At kilometre 5 (mile 3.1) on this road is a little brown sign on the left side. Immediately after the Adams Lake Road is a road off the pavement. This road leads into the parking lot for the Flume Trail. There are a number of trails here and they all have steep sections. You will walk beside the Hiuihill Creek, through tall, shady trees, and across bridges. There are signs telling you where you are and how to get onto other trails. Watch for remnants of the old flume used to send logs down the mountainside.

Back at the Adams Lake turn-off, if you continue down the road past Haig-Brown Provincial Park towards Shuswap Lake Provincial Park, you will

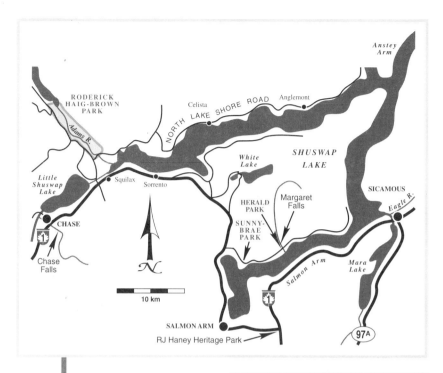

follow the north shore of Shuswap Lake. A number of towns along the shore feature several kinds of crafts by local people. Visitors may stop in at some studios so watch for the signs. Seymour Arm, the furthest town on the road, at the north end of Shuswap Lake, is the site of Ogden City, an old gold rush town.

Flume Hiking Trail

SALMON SPAWNING

Salmon return each September and October to spawn in the Adams River. Every fourth year is a dominant year while the next year is considered sub-dominant and the other two are fairly quiet.

The fish journey almost 650 kilometres (400 miles) from the Pacific Ocean, up the Fraser and Thompson Rivers to Adams River. The spawning beds are protected but you can walk beside the river or sit on a bench to watch the fish swimming past.

SQUILAX AND SORRENTO

Squilax General Store

Back once again heading east on Highway 1 you round a curve and there is the Squilax Store. It is an old, faded, red brick building and the floors inside are shiplap. The cabooses set amongst the trees below the store are the Squilax Hostel – you can register at the store.

A few kilometres east on Highway 1 is Sorrento, originally known as Trapper's Landing because it was the meeting place of the Shuswap trappers who came here with their furs. In the early 1900s the name was changed because a man, John Kinghorn, said Copper Island reminded him of the Isle of Capri off Sorrento, Italy. Copper Island is out in Shuswap Lake, just off the shore at Sorrento, and is only accessible by boat.

Sorrento is home to the annual Shuswap Lake Festival of the Arts. It is held over nine days in July and features the works of artists and artisans from the Shuswap area.

The Native peoples believe mythical creatures live in the Shuswap Lake and stories

Squilax Hostel

White Post Auto Museum

have been told about them for centuries. Shuswap Lake is great for windsurfing and char, trout, salmon, Dolly Varden and rainbow trout are waiting for the angler. There are a great number of resort towns along the lakeshore.

At kilometre 15.7 (mile 9.8) from Sorrento is the White Post Auto Museum. Take a tour through it. There are 40 restored vehicles inside, many of which are for sale or trade. Outside in the compound are vehicles that need restoring. You might find something of interest.

Two kilometres (1.2 miles) from the museum is the road to Sunnybrae and Herald provincial parks, a lovely drive along the shore of Shuswap Lake. Shortly after the turn you reach Sunnybrae Provincial Park. Herald Provincial Park is on the right at kilometre 11.2 (mile 7). Just past the entrance is the parking lot for Margaret Falls on your left. This is a popular falls so you might have to park on the road.

Trail to Margaret Falls

Margaret Falls

The easy 15 minute hike in to the falls takes you through a canyon surrounded by tall trees and rock walls. It is cool and damp and dim. Bridges are over the creek and sometimes you have to duck under trees that have fallen over the path. The waterfall is two tiered so you won't get it all in one picture.

The people of the area called these falls Reinecker Falls after the family who first owned the property. Then the land was purchased by a Dr. Herald, and Reinecker Falls was renamed Margaret Falls, after the first non-Native woman to visit their waters.

SALMON ARM

In Salmon Arm, the nature centre and the tourist information building are on Marine Park Drive. Signs are posted. At Nature Bay you will find a long boardwalk out into the wetland, two bird blinds and two nature trails. One trail leads from the centre office and the other begins across the street. No dogs are allowed on the paths so as not to scare the birds.

In the spring, the Salmon River deposits silt in this bay leaving a large, rich, marsh. In the summer, the lake rises, covering the marsh. Fish fry, along with insects and plants, attract migratory birds to the area. The waters are home to the largest colony of western grebe in British Columbia. There are over 150 different species of birds and waterfowl in the marsh.

If you are here around the middle of September, take in the Salmon Arm Fall Fair. It is full of displays of vegetables, field crops, preserves, wine, home baking, farm and exotic animals, exhibits of photography, and crafts. There is a parade, a horse pull with heavy and miniature horses, and a midway. This fair has been a tradition since 1898.

Salmon Arm Nature Bay

Church at Haney Heritage Park

Just east of Salmon Arm is the junction with Highway 97B. Turn right onto it and in a quarter of a kilometre (a sixth of a mile) you will reach the R.J. Haney Heritage Park. In the park is the Haney farmhouse, built in 1910, and the Mount Ida Church, constructed in 1911 and recently moved to the park. There are nature paths, a museum and an old school. The Annual Salmon Arm Bluegrass Festival is held here each July and bands come from western Canada, the USA and even Russia to participate.

SICAMOUS TO THREE VALLEY GAP

SICAMOUS

Follow Highway 1 along the lakeshore to Sicamous. As you cross the bridge into Sicamous look to your right and you will see the rows of houseboats waiting to be rented. Sicamous, on the eastern side of Shuswap Lake and the northern end of Mara Lake, is known as 'the Houseboat Capital of Canada.' Over 300 vessels are docked in the channel at Sicamous.

You can rent a houseboat to explore the lakes or take a cruise on the *Phoebe Ann*, a replica of the sternwheelers that plied many lakes and rivers of the province before the railway. For information, stop in at the Shuswap Lake Ferry Service at the end of Finlayson Street, the most northerly street in town.

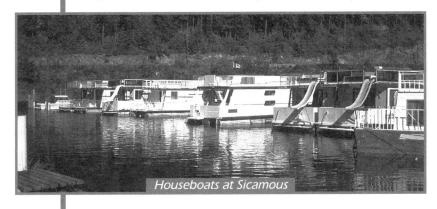
Houseboats at Sicamous

Sicamous Lake

If you are out on the lake and run out of food, the General Store is north of Sicamous where Anstey Arm joins the lake. The store is in the log cabin floating on the water.

Fishing is great on the Shuswap. Many giant rainbow trout have been caught over the years, with the largest being 13.6 kilograms (30 pounds), caught back in 1949. In April 1995 a 9.8 kilogram (21 pound 8 ounce), 86 centimetre (34 inch) rainbow was caught near Marble Point.

Wallabies at D Dutchman Dairy

The Red Barn on Riverside Avenue has bingo games Sunday or Thursday evenings and Saturday morning. Also on Saturday at the barn is the Indoor Market where you can purchase fruit, vegetables and home baking, or browse through the flea market.

Pattullo Gardens

As you head east out of Sicamous, stop in at D Dutchman Dairy on Maier Road. You have to make a sharp right-hand turn. You can take a self-guided tour of the dairy, which produces milk, cheese and ice cream. And speaking of ice cream, 59 different flavours tempt your palate. Outside in the yard is a small zoo with wallabies, a camel, a llama and birds.

Eleven kilometres (6.8 miles) east of Sicamous is the turn into Pattullo Gardens. You drive back parallel to the highway to get to the parking lot. A map at the beginning explains where to go to see certain sites such as the giant cedars, display gardens and the Eagle River. There are old buildings and machinery, a nursery and snack bar. Come here in the spring for your bedding plants if you live nearby.

CRAIGELLACHIE

Craigellachie is where, on November 7, 1885, the 'Last Spike' of the Canadian Pacific Railway was driven. This spike marked the completion of the approximately 4800 kilometres (3000 miles) of track that spanned Canada from the Atlantic to the Pacific. To commemorate this occasion, a small park has been set up on the site, which has a cairn, a caboose, a section of track and a gift shop.

Look carefully at the base of the cairn. In it is a rock brought over

Last Spike, Craigellachie

from Craigellachie, Scotland, as well as a rock from each province and territory in Canada. Walk around the cairn and read the plaques over each rock telling which province or territory it came from. This site is operated by the Revelstoke Railway Museum.

Miniatureland

Miniatureland is 16 kilometres (10 miles) east of the Last Spike. You cross the Perry River and turn left. There is a short climb up to the parking lot. Inside, everything is in miniature. The Swiss Pavillion, with a Swiss mountain village and cable cars, and the German Pavilion, with a medieval-style town, are at a scale of 1:25. There is a display of the Craigellachie railway station and train engine, a prairie town and characters from Mother Goose nursery rhymes. There are hundreds of hand-made exhibits and Canada's largest animated toyland display. Just push the button and watch the toys move.

FISHING WITHOUT A LICENCE

If you want to try fishing but haven't bought a licence yet, stop in at the Mal-Aqua Culture, just east of Miniatureland, where you can catch your own trout from the U-catch pond. No fishing licence is required and rods and bait are on site.

You can cook your fish yourself over the barbecues or take it home with you. Or, if you wish, you can just stop in to buy some smoked trout and arctic char. Mal-Aqua is a fish farm with a hatchery and growing ponds but no tours.

Your children will love the Enchanted Forest about 10 km (6 miles) east of Miniatureland. Along the paths through the forest are over 250 hand-crafted figures from fairy tales and nursery rhymes. For the adults there is an old-growth forest. Stand inside a hollow giant, or climb another. Some cedars, spared both by fire and by humans, are over 600 years old. The hulking burnt shells you see were left by a fire in the late 1800s.

Don't worry if it's raining when you come; free umbrellas are supplied on overcast days.

THREE VALLEY GAP

Watch for the red-and-white reflection of the Three Valley Gap Hotel in the waters of Three Valley Lake. This hotel is a modern resort that offers stage shows and great dining. It was built near where the original town of Three Valley grew and died in the late 1880s. Outside in the yard is an historic town with over 20 old buildings.

Three Valley Gap Hotel

If you are on your honeymoon, stay in the Cave Room. Its whole interior is constructed from stone. Visit the Walter Moberly Theatre and listen to Canadian cowboy stories and yodelling, and watch some fancy rope work.

EAGLE PASS

In August of 1865, Walter Moberly, a government surveyor, was looking for a route through the Monashee Mountains. He watched an eagle fly through a low pass and followed it. On August 29th he stood on top of Mount Moody. To the left he could see the Columbia River; to the right, Shuswap Lake. He named the waters below him 'Lake of the Three Valleys,' and the pass he had discovered, 'Eagle Pass.'

As you are crossing the CPR railway tracks at kilometre 8 (mile 5) from Three Valley Gap, look to your left and you will see a row of three train tunnels across Summit Lake.

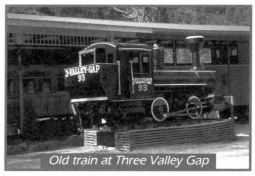
Old train at Three Valley Gap

These three tunnels, which are 118, 75 and 70 metres (386, 247 and 229 feet) in length, were built by some of the Chinese workers brought in by the railway to work on the tracks across the mountains. They were finished in 1884.

REVELSTOKE TO GOLDEN

REVELSTOKE

As you enter Revelstoke from the west you cross the Columbia River. North of Revelstoke on Highway 23, also known as the Big Bend Highway, there are two dams, Revelstoke and Mica, on this part of the mighty Columbia River.

Revelstoke Dam

Revelstoke Dam is 8 kilometres (5 miles) from the junction with Highway 1. It has a parking area and a visitors' centre where you can take a self-guided tour, the highlight of which is an elevator trip up to the top of the 175 metre (574 foot) high concrete dam. This is Canada's highest concrete dam.

Formed by the dam is Lake Revelstoke, which you will follow all the way north to Mica Dam. Lake Revelstoke has Gerrard rainbow trout and bull trout. You should use heavier tackle to catch them and troll deep with minnow-imitating plugs. There are recreation sites, boat launches, picnic areas, viewpoints, and splendid scenery along the way.

The one service station on this road is at kilometre 74 (mile 46), and you have to turn onto Wallis Road to reach it.

COLUMBIA RIVER

At 1954 kilometres (1214 miles), the Columbia River is the longest river on the Pacific seaboard. It drains 100,000 square kilometres (38,500 square miles) and has 14 dams along its length in Canada and the United States. The river is the largest hydroelectric producer in the world.

The Columbia River leaves Columbia Lake near Fairmont Hot Springs. It flows north for over 300 kilometres (185 miles) into Kinbasket Lake formed by the Mica Dam on the river north of Revelstoke. When it leaves that lake it immediately becomes Lake Revelstoke because of the Revelstoke Dam.

The river heads south for over 400 kilometres (250 miles) to the border. Just south of Revelstoke, it widens to form the Upper and Lower Arrow Lakes which, because of their immense size, keep winter temperatures mild in the area. They also contribute to the retention of moisture in the air and therefore to the type of vegetation growing in the area and the crops that grow well there.

The river crosses into Washington just south of Trail and flows to its mouth at Astoria, Oregon.

There is a ferry that will take you to the other side of the lake, where there are campsites, at kilometre 137 (mile 85). Continue along the east side of the lake past Mica Creek, where there are no services, to reach Mica Dam at kilometre 146 (mile 91).

The top of Mica Dam is 200 metres (650 feet) above the river. It is surrounded by the Rocky, Selkirk and Monashee Mountains. Free guided tours of the underground powerhouse are offered at 11 am and 1:30 pm. There is no overnight camping at the dam.

Mica Dam formed the huge reservoir, Kinbasket Lake, which was named after Shuswap Chief Kinbasket. He was hired as a guide by David Thompson on his explorations through the area. The reservoir was filled in 1976 and it stretches about 215 kilometres (135 miles) from Valemount, near Mount Robson Park, to Donald Station, just north of Golden. It covers an area of around 42,500 hectares (105,000 acres).

The town of Revelstoke was established in 1880 under the name of Farwell. It was a railway town and was renamed after Lord Revelstoke, the head of a London bank that loaned funds for the completion of the Canadian Pacific Railway. In 1889 Revelstoke was appointed a mountain divisional centre for the railway and it is still a railway town. The railway museum has many displays of the town's railway history as well as exhibits of logging and river-boating. Take the time to visit the art gallery above the museum.

Mica Dam

Piano Keep, Revelstoke

A place you must see is the Piano Keep, which has pianos dating from 1783 to 1905. At the set of lights just after you cross the bridge over the Columbia River turn right onto Victoria and drive down to MacKenzie Avenue. (You will pass the railway museum, which is on Pearson Street.) At the stop sign there are two big bears on your right. Drive between them onto MacKenzie and continue to Seventh Street. The Piano Keep is in the huge, three-storey Edwardian house on the corner. The first-floor rooms of this 1905 home are full of the old pianos. Look up the flight of stairs and see the picture painted on the wall at the landing. Tours are offered at 1 pm and 3 pm during July and August. Incidentally, the house is also a bed-and-breakfast.

MOUNT REVELSTOKE NATIONAL PARK

If you want to climb to the summit of a mountain without much effort, or see an alpine meadow with the mountain tops across the valley as a backdrop, then turn onto the Mount Revelstoke Summit Drive just as you head east out of town. You have to be in the right lane to make the turn around a curve to go under the highway and head north. It costs a small fee to drive the 26 kilometre (16 mile) road to the Meadows in the Sky at the summit of the 1938 metre (6358 foot) high Mount Revelstoke. This road is full of switchbacks and is one of the few roads where you can drive through

Flowers growing at high altitudes

the forests of the interior wet belt right up to alpine meadows. At the parking lot you can either walk the half kilometre (third of a mile) to the meadow or take the shuttle operated by the park.

The Meadows in the Sky Trail is a 1 kilometre (0.6 mile) loop. The best time to see the flowers is at the beginning of August, when the blossoms are at their height. It can be an unusual experience to see flowers growing at your feet and then to look across the valley at the mountain peaks around you.

To reach the very top of Mount Revelstoke, take the asphalt path beside the welcome signs and start climbing. It is quite steep but takes only about five minutes. At the top is the summit sign, still measured in Imperial feet, and a historic fire lookout. From here you look down on everything. Because of the altitude, on a cool or rainy day you should take an extra jacket.

Back on Highway 1, about 18 kilometres (11 miles) east of Revelstoke, you find that you are driving through Mount Revelstoke National Park. Your first stop is the Skunk Cabbage Boardwalk. There is a picnic area and a 1.2 kilometre (0.7 mile) trail that takes you along the Illecillewaet River, past a viewpoint, and on a boardwalk through the Skunk Cabbage Marsh. This marsh is great for birdwatching as the swampy area is a popular site for the neotropical thrushes, flycatchers and warblers. These are just a few of the birds that migrate to the tropics of Central and South America to avoid our winters. They return here in the spring to nest.

Mount Revelstoke summit

Giant Cedars Boardwalk

Just past the marsh you come to the Giant Cedars Boardwalk and this is a must see. It is so serene to walk through the 1000-year-old giant redcedar and hemlock trees. Inhale deeply as you stroll on the boardwalk in the alternating shade created by the overhead branches and sunlight that manages to filter through. A creek bubbles by, making the scene complete.

Western redcedars and western hemlocks in this area can have a diameter of 2.4 metres (7.9 feet) and a circumference of 7.7 metres (25 feet). This is a damp forest area, very different from the montane forests of the lower Rocky Mountains. You will also find thimbleberry, falsebox, devil's club and ferns on your walk.

CANYON HOT SPRINGS

There are two entrances for Canyon Hot Springs, which is about 5 kilometres (3 miles) east of Mount Revelstoke National Park. Water for the 68,000 litre (15,000 gallon), 40°C (104°F) hot pool and the 272,000 litre (60,000 gallon) 27°C (80°F) swimming pool is piped 3.2 kilometres (2 miles) from the mountains. You can swim in the cooler pool or just lay back in the hot pool and enjoy the mountain scenery around you. There is an RV park here so you can spend a couple of days.

At kilometre 10.7 (mile 6.6) east of Canyon Hot Springs you come to the first of

Canyon Hot Springs

three avalanche control tunnels built over the highway. Keep your headlights on through these tunnels because visibility is limited.

GLACIER NATIONAL PARK

Glacier National Park is in the northern Selkirk Range of the Columbia Mountains and is the meeting place of two weather systems. Moist Pacific air keeps the western area mild in the winter, while the eastern part is kept cold and dry by the continental weather. Over 1450 millimetres (57 inches) of precipitation falls each year. There is a 50% chance of rain every day in the summer and a 100% chance of snow every day in the winter. This heavy fall keeps the more than 400 active glaciers and icepacks in the area supplied with snow.

PLANT LIFE

There are three biogeoclimatic zones in Glacier National Park. At the valley bottom is the Interior Cedar–Hemlock Zone with its dense rainforest of western white pine, Douglas-fir, water hemlock, western red cedar and white birch. People interested in plants will want to check the creeks and rivers for water-hemlock, skunk cabbage, alder and sedges, which are rare in the Selkirks.

In the middle zone of Engelmann Spruce–Subalpine fir, the lower part has the spruce and fir as well as mountain hemlock, while the upper part has only small clumps of subalpine fir. However the undergrowth is brightly coloured with Indian paintbrush, fireweed, glacier lily and Sitka valerian.

In spite of the harsh weather and short growing season, there is nevertheless vegetation even in the Alpine Tundra Zone: lichens, sedges, heathers and Sitka valerian.

Just inside Glacier National Park is the Hemlock Grove Boardwalk. The 400-metre (1300 feet) walk is lovely and cool on a hot day. It takes you through the hemlock trees and the smells of the forest are so good.

Hemlock Grove, Glacier National Park

Rogers Pass Summit

Back on the highway, you periodically see metal, square platforms with a pedestal in the centre. They are for the big Howitzer guns that are used to control avalanches by dislodging unstable snowpacks while the highway is closed.

The crossing of the Beaver River is just above the entrance to the CPR's 8 kilometre (5 mile) Connaught Tunnel, which travels through Mount Macdonald. This tunnel was the longest in Canada when built. It was completed in 1916 to cut out the steep grades and avoid the avalanches. In 1988 the Mount Macdonald Tunnel was built to replace the earlier tunnel; at 14.7 kilometres (9 miles) it is now the longest in North America.

The Rogers Pass Summit is at 1330 metres (4363 feet) above sea level. An arch beside the highway on the left marks the summit. With the snow-capped mountains behind, it makes a great picture. The asphalt path just east of the arch is the Abandoned Rails Trail to the information centre. The 1.3 kilometre (0.8 mile) trail follows along part of an old rail bed, abandoned in 1916 because of too many avalanche disasters.

ROGERS PASS

In 1871 British Columbia joined Canada with the understanding that a railway would be built across the mountains to connect the new province with the rest of the country. The Canadian Pacific Railway was brought west across the open prairies, through the Bow River valley and over Kicking Horse Pass in the Rocky Mountains. But at the Columbia River the only choice seemed to be to take the tracks up the 'Big Bend' of the river, which meant going around the mountains.

Although men had searched for a route through the Selkirk Mountains for years none had been found. finally in 1881 a railway surveyor named Rogers made it to the headwaters of the Illecillewaet River and the pass he crossed was later named for him. Thanks to him, the railway was completed in 1885.

Winters were a bad time for the trains: avalanches blocked the tracks for hours or days. Sometimes a second avalanche would cascade down the slopes, catching the rail-clearing crew by surprise.

Abandoned Rails Trail

On March 4, 1910 an avalanche from Cheops Mountain had spewed snow and debris onto the tracks and a crew was sent out to clear them. Soon after they started work, a second avalanche buried them, killing 62 men. Although many men had been lost in other avalanches since 1885, this was the one that made the CPR look for an alternate route west.

Just 1 kilometre (0.6 mile) from the arch is the Rogers Pass Information Centre with exhibits showing the area's history and geology, and outdoor displays. Also at the summit is a restaurant, service station and hotel. If you run out of film taking pictures of the mountains, you can pick some more up here.

Just over 2 kilometres (1.2 miles) from the summit you come to six more avalanche tunnels. Remember to use your headlights.

Kilometre 23 (mile 14.3) from the summit is where the time zone changes, so set your watches and clocks ahead one hour.

Although the CPR had been through the pass since 1885, building of the Trans-Canada Highway didn't begin until 1956. Construction was halted time and again by snowslides, and the steep grades caused many headaches. Because of these challenges, the highway didn't open until 1962.

From Glacier National Park to Golden, sit back and enjoy the scenery.

INDEX

A

B

C

G

H

I

J

K

FURTHER READING

Barman, Jean. *The West Beyond the West.* Toronto: University of Toronto Press, 1991.

Beers, Don. *The Wonder of Yoho.* Calgary: Rocky Mountain Books, 1989.

Bowers, Dan. *Exploring the Southern Okanagan.* Vancouver: Douglas & McIntyre, 1978.

Bryan, Liz and Jack Bryan. *Country Roads.* Vancouver: Sunflower Publications Ltd., 1991.

The Canadian Encyclopedia. Second Edition. Edmonton: Hurtig, 1988.

Chalmers, J.W. *Fur Trade Governor.* Edmonton: Institute of Applied Art Ltd., 1960.

Dodd, John and Gail Helgason. *Canadian Rockies Access Guide.* Edmonton: Lone Pine Publishing, 1987.

Downs, Art, editor. *Pioneer Days in British Columbia.* Volumes I and II. Surrey: Hertiage House Publishing Co., Ltd., 1975, 1979.

Gibson, Nancy and John Whittaker. *Lone Pine Picnic Guide to British Columbia.* Edmonton: Lone Pine Publishing, 1989.

Harris, Bob. *The Best of B.C. Hiking Trails.* Vancouver: Special Interest Publications, 1986.

Kramer, Pat. *B.C. For Free.* Vancouver: Whitecap Books, 1992.

DISCOVER BRITISH COLUMBIA
WITH Lone Pine Publishing!

Hiking the Ancient Forests
of British Columbia and Washington
by *Randy Stoltmann*

Celebrate the few remaining old-growth forests of British Columbia and Washington. Fascinating and captivating stories blend with useful information on hiking through these magnificent stands of mammoth trees. The hikes described in this book range from easy, short walks near urban areas to overnight backpacking trips in more remote areas. Even if you never leave your armchair, this book will help you become better informed about our diminishing ancient forests.

5.5" x 8.5" • 192 pages • maps throughout • 90 B&W photographs •
Softcover • $19.95 CDN • $15.95 US • ISBN 1-55105-045-5

Plants of Southern Interior British Columbia
by *Roberta Parish, Ray Coupé* and *Dennis Lloyd*

Plants of Southern Interior British Columbia provides nature enthusiasts with detailed descriptions of over 675 species of trees, shrubs, wildflowers, grasses, ferns, mosses and lichens. With 1000 color photographs, and 700 illustrations, *Plants of Southern Interior British Columbia* is also easy to use, and invaluable for your next foray into nature. Learn more about the world outside your door with Lone Pine's Plant Field Guides.

5.5" x 8.5" • 454 pages • 1000 color photographs • 700 illustrations •
Softcover • $24.95 CDN • $19.95 US • ISBN 1-55105-057-9

Trees, Shrubs and Flowers To Know
in British Columbia and Washington
by *C.P. Lyons* and *Bill Merilees*

Chess Lyons has updated his classic guide on British Columbia and Washington for today's naturalists and nature enthusiasts. This guide identifies more than 600 common trees, shrubs and flowers with line drawings, tree distribution maps and a wildflower guide with over 400 photographs.

5.5" x 8.5" • 376 pages • 59 maps • 446 color photographs •
over 600 line drawings • Softcover • $18.95 CDN • $15.95 US
ISBN 1-55105-044-7

LONE PINE PUBLISHING

206, 10426-81 Avenue	202A, 1110 Seymour Street	16149 Redmond Way, #180
Edmonton, Alberta	Vancouver, British Columbia	Redmond, Washington
Canada T6E 1X5	Canada V6B 3N3	U.S.A. 98052

LONE
PINE

PHONE 1-800-661-9017   **FAX 1-800-424-7173**